Moral Minority

ALSO BY BROOKE ALLEN

Twentieth-Century Attitudes
Artistic License

MORAL MINORITY

Our Skeptical Founding Fathers

Brooke Allen

Ivan R. Dee   Chicago

The chapter "Jefferson" was first published in *The Hudson Review*.

www.ivanrdee.com

The paperback edition of this book carries the ISBN 1-56663-751-1.

Library of Congress Cataloging-in-Publication Data:
Allen, Brooke.
    Moral minority : our skeptical founding fathers / Brooke Allen.
        p. cm.
    Includes bibliographical references and index.
    ISBN-13: 978-1-56663-675-9 (cloth : alk. paper)
    ISBN-10: 1-56663-675-2 (cloth : alk. paper)
        1. Church and state—United States—History—18th century. 2. Freedom of religion—United States—History—18th century. 3. Religion and politics—United States—History—18th century. 4. Christianity and politics—United States—History—18th century. 5. United States—Religion—To 1800. 6. Statesmen—Religious life—United States—History—18th century. 7. Statesmen—United States—Biography. I. Title.
    BR516.A46 2006
    277.3'07—dc22   2006008160

To Brian and Sidney Urquhart

Acknowledgments

I WOULD LIKE to give thanks to Katrina vanden Heuvel and Victor Navasky, who published the original article from which this book grew in *The Nation*, and to the excellent editors I worked with at that magazine.

My greatest debt is to the many friends who spent time talking with me about the ideas that arose during the composition of this book, and helped me to direct and refine my thoughts. Edmund Leites read an early version of the manuscript and gave me very valuable advice on how to change and improve the book's structure. Two other *real* historians, Drew Gilpin Faust and David Nasaw, also gave helpful suggestions, as did Michael Anderson, David Grubin, Lisa Aaron, and Roelfien Kuijpers. A number of others gave me the benefit of their thoughts on these subjects: Brian and Sidney Urquhart, Bill Pepper, Bill Eiland, Andrew Ladis, Ed Harte, Andrew Aaron, and Patrick Doyle.

I owe a great deal of gratitude to my husband, Peter Aaron; my daughters, Eve and Elizabeth Aaron; and my mother, Jay Allen, for their continued enthusiasm and support.

My father, who died in 2003, was a firm skeptic who came from a long line of freethinkers, to judge by their names: our ancestors in Virginia included men called David Hume Allen, Algernon Sidney Allen, and Robert Owen Allen. So I suppose I have come by my interests naturally.

Contents

Preface

THE IDEA FOR THIS BOOK came in 2004, when our president and various current and past members of the United States government could be heard on almost any given day, on television or the radio, asserting that this nation was founded on Christian principles (or sometimes, as a sop to the Jewish constituency, Judeo-Christian principles). This seemed to me so demonstrably untrue that a strong refutation was called for. It is true that *some* of the original colonists fled Europe for religious reasons; it is true that *some* of the first colonies were founded as religious communities; it is even true that most of the men who signed the Declaration of Independence and the Constitution were practicing Christians of one denomination or another. Nevertheless this nation was *not* founded on Christian principles.

The very multiplicity of sects and the diverse religious backgrounds of the original colonists ensured that it would be practically impossible to come up with a religious settlement for the new nation that everyone could agree on. Religion, like slavery, was a topic so divisive as to threaten orderly government and any chance of creating an inclusive constitution. Hence the policy finally arrived at by the architects of the Constitution and the Bill of Rights: to keep religion,

Christian and otherwise, entirely out of the legal framework of the United States. Therefore there is no reference to God in the Constitution, and religion is mentioned only for the purposes of ensuring its absence in government: "No religious test shall ever be required as a qualification to any office or public trust under the United States," and "Congress shall make no law respecting an establishment of religion, or prohibiting the free exercise thereof." The brief mentions of "our Creator" and "Nature and Nature's God" in the Declaration of Independence were specifically formulated to apply not just to Christians but to adherents of all religions, including non-Christian ones. It will be noticed that Jesus Christ's name appears nowhere in these documents; this was not an accidental omission.

When he was asked why there was no mention of God in the Constitution, Alexander Hamilton flippantly answered, "We forgot." Of course, as his biographer Ron Chernow has pointed out, Hamilton never forgot anything important. John Adams expressed his own religious creed "in four short Words 'Be just and good.'" It is to this broadest possible definition of faith that the Founding Fathers were appealing, and they included even "infidels," a dirty word at the time, in their concept of a unified civil community.

But what, Christian apologists will say, about our mottoes "In God We Trust" and "One Nation Under God?" The answer is that these were not created by the Founding Fathers but were inventions of later, more pious times. "In God We Trust" was put on our coins at a moment of religious remorse after the Civil War, and "One Nation Under God" added to the Pledge of Allegiance during the McCarthy hysteria of the 1950s.

The more I thought about all of this, and the more I read, the more obvious it became that the key Founding Fathers were not strictly orthodox believers and in many cases not even Christians at all. They were broad-minded intellectuals, clear products of the international Enlightenment. As such, they tended to see religious zeal as an irrational, divisive, and even atavistic passion that constituted a threat to human society. Open-minded and latitudinarian themselves, they sought to remove such zeal from the federal legislature and keep it where it belonged: in church.

In 2005 I wrote an article on this subect for *The Nation*, called "Our Godless Constitution"—a title borrowed from Isaac Kramnick and R. Laurence Moore's wonderful 1997 study. But the subject still would not leave me alone, and this book is the result.

Most Americans seem to be under an erroneous impression, given by teachers, preachers, textbooks, and pundits, that the Founding Fathers were pious bores. So it is time to talk clearly about them as they really were: not the good Christians our teachers droned on about, but skeptical men of the Enlightenment who questioned each and every received idea they had been taught. They were deeply read in political philosophy, interested in science, and well versed in theological matters. They consistently challenged the religious dogma they heard from the pulpit, both openly and in private, among friends. Thomas Jefferson urged his young nephew to subject the authors of the New Testament to the same textual scrutiny he would give to other ancient historians like Tacitus or Livy, and to treat supposed biblical miracles with particular suspicion. For himself, he edited a version of the New Testament that left out every miraculous and supernatural occurrence, leaving only Jesus' moral injunctions. George Washington rewrote the presidential addresses crafted for him by others so as to omit all references to Jesus Christ. James Madison gave it as his opinion that "Religious bondage shackles and debilitates the mind and unfits it for every noble enterprize every expanded project."

The eighteenth century was not an age of faith but an age of science and skepticism, and the American Founding Fathers were in its vanguard. As the philosopher Louis Dupré has uncompromisingly stated, "Our [Western] institutions and laws, our conception of the state, and our political sensitivity all stem from Enlightenment ideas. This, of course, is particularly true in the United States, where the

Founding Fathers transformed those ideas into an unsurpassed system of balanced government." Even to their contemporaries this seemed obvious: the American Revolution, and the subsequent creation of the United States, embodied the Enlightenment values that had been formulated over the previous century. The American experiment was an Enlightenment experiment. While some (though certainly not all) of the American colonies had originally been founded as religious communities—the Massachusetts Bay colony, chartered in 1629, was the major example of this sort of scheme—the ultimate confederation of the thirteen very different colonies as the United States of America was a purely secular project. The absence of God in the new nation's Constitution was a highly deliberate, indeed a vital part of that project.

There were many reasons for this omission, but two trumped all the others. First, the terrible religious wars and massacres that had followed the European Reformation were a part of recent history, and it was a history from which the Founding Fathers were determined to divert the new nation's course. Many of them had sprung from religious populations that had emigrated to the New World in order to escape brutal persecution at home: English Puritans and Catholics, Quakers, French Huguenots, and other dissenters from the established churches of Europe. Second, the very number and variety of sects in the American colonies guaranteed that it would be difficult if not impossible to invent and impose a satisfactory religious settlement. Individual colonies had established churches—Anglican (Episcopalian) in Virginia, for example, and Congregational (Calvinist) in the New England states—but the dissenting denominations were gaining in numbers and clout and challenging the established ones with increasing frequency. The thought of uniting all these disparate sects under one national church was clearly a challenge no one was willing to face.

The Founding Fathers who gathered at the First and Second Continental Congresses and ultimately at the Constitutional Convention of 1787, though undoubtedly provincial, were educated men of the international Enlightenment. Almost half of the signers of the Declaration of Independence, for example, were lawyers, and a very large proportion were college graduates—this at a time when higher education was not yet widespread and when the status of college graduate implied a much higher level of education than it does today. This was also true of the signers of the Constitution. Most of them were practicing Christians, to be sure, but many others, including some of the most influential and important, were skeptics, deists, and agnostics. Their primary concern was to establish a strong civil society with protected rights for its citizens. Religion, most of them believed, was a personal matter which should be forcibly kept out of the public arena. The man who had the greatest single influence on the United States Constitution was not Jesus Christ but John Locke.

To understand the social, intellectual, and religious climate our Founding Fathers came out of, the reader may turn to Chapter Eight. There, key terms like Deism, Calvinism, and Latitudinarianism are explained as they relate to our founders and to the political world they created, and the chaotic religious background within the thirteen colonies is clarified; the story of the religious struggles in England, from which so many of the founders' families had fled, is also told. But my primary motive in writing this book was to tell some personal stories about the Founding Fathers and their attitudes toward religion in general, and Christianity in particular. The main portion of the book, therefore, is made up of short religious histories of the six men whom I considered the principal Founding Fathers: Benjamin Franklin, George Washington, John Adams, Thomas Jefferson, James Madison, and Alexander Hamilton. This is not to demean the enormous contributions made by so many others, such as Benjamin Rush, John Jay, James Otis, Samuel Adams, William Livingston, Edmund Randolph, Thomas Paine, Gouverneur Morris, Richard Henry Lee, and John Hancock. It is just that the six I have chosen are the iconic ones. These six men are the ones whose faces we see on our bills and our coins, whose portraits are engraved in our memories; they are the ones we name our elementary schools and our streets and our cities after; they are the ones we learn about, or think we learn about, as schoolchildren.

These men were not advocates for a monolithic notion of "God and Country," as promoters of a Christian America would now have us believe. They were precisely the opposite: the very prototypes, in fact, of the East Coast intellectuals we are always being warned against by today's religious right.

Moral Minority

CHAPTER ONE

Franklin

⚡ BENJAMIN FRANKLIN was one of the great figures of the international Enlightenment, revered in France even more, if possible, than he was in his native land. When he arrived in Paris in 1776 as American minister to France, his highly-publicized experiments in electricity and countless other fields had earned him a place as perhaps the foremost scientist of the age. There he was greeted rapturously by his fellow *philosophes* and the *salonnières* who patronized them. The French statesman Turgot voiced the general opinion when he claimed that Franklin had "snatched lightning from the sky and the scepter from tyrants." Immanuel Kant dubbed him "the new Prometheus"; David Hume lauded him as America's "first philosopher" and "first great man of letters." The adulation poured upon him by the European intelligentsia equaled that accorded to Voltaire, and the staged meeting of the two philosopher-kings was one of the emblematic moments of the eighteenth century. It was amusingly described by Franklin's grumpy colleague John Adams:

> There presently arose a general cry that M. Voltaire and
> M. Franklin should be introduced to each other. This was
> done, and they bowed and spoke to each other. This was no

satisfaction; there must be something more. Neither of our philosophers seemed to divine what was wished or expected; they however took each other by the hand. But this was not enough. The clamor continued until the explanation came out: Il faut s'embrasser a la francaise. The two aged actors upon this great theater of philosophy and frivolity then embraced each other by hugging one another in their arms and kissing each other's cheeks, and then the tumult subsided. And the cry immediately spread through the kingdom, and I suppose all over Europe: Qu'il est charmant de voir embrasser Solon et Sophocle.

The toast of France's intellectuals and would-be intellectuals, Franklin consorted not only with Voltaire, whose name at that time was a byword for atheism, but with all the other most famous skeptics of the time: Mirabeau, d'Holbach, d'Alembert, Buffon, and Condorcet. All these men were generally referred to as "freethinkers," a term used to describe those who rejected the "leap of faith" necessary to accept revealed religion, instead subjecting religious claims to empirical examination. They took him, possibly correctly, for one of themselves, and a French acquaintance claimed that "our free-thinkers have adroitly sounded him on his religion, and they maintain that he is one of their own, that is that he has none at all."

Adams, who knew Franklin well, seems to have agreed, at least if we are to credit this 1779 excerpt from his diary:

> "All religions are tolerated in America," said M. Marbois [the Marquis François de Barbé-Marbois]; "and the ambassadors have in all courts a right to a chapel in their own way; but Mr. Franklin never had any." "No," said I, laughing, "because Mr. Franklin had no—" I was going to say what I did not say, and will not say here. I stopped short, and laughed. "No," said M. Marbois; "Mr. Franklin adores only great Nature, which has interested a great many people of both sexes in his favor."

"Yes," said I, laughing, "all the atheists, deists, and libertines, as well as the philosophers and ladies, are in his train,— another Voltaire, and thence—" "Yes," said M. Marbois, "he is celebrated as the great philosopher and the great legislator of America."

Franklin may, certainly, have been an atheist. If he was one, he was enough of a politician and diplomat never to have committed himself to that dangerous position, or to have recorded it in writing. But if one defines a Christian as someone who believes in the divinity of Jesus Christ, Franklin could not be called a Christian. If it were necessary to place him in a category, he could perhaps be classified as a deist—someone who believes in the existence of a higher being but in little else—though he found even that loosest of denominations too constricting to formally adopt. Deists did not believe in the Trinity or Christ's divinity, and many orthodox believers of the time tended dismissively to equate them with atheists. But Franklin took good care to differentiate the two, as in this 1747 letter: "I oppose *my theist* [deist] to [the] *atheist*, because I think they are diametrically opposite; and not near of kin, as Mr. [George] Whitefield seems to suppose, where, (in his Journal) he tells us *"Mr. B. was a deist, I had almost said an atheist;'* that is, *chalk*, I had almost said *charcoal."*

As a man of the Enlightenment, Franklin was keenly interested in religion as a branch, as it were, of anthropology, but he attached himself to no particular creed. The historian Henry F. May expressed it in a wonderfully blunt manner when he said that Franklin's "observations of Quakers, Dunkards, Baptists, Jews, and Catholics are recorded in the tone of a friendly, but quite uninvolved, student of comparative religion or, less attractively, in that of a rising businessman and politician who sees no point in making enemies over unimportant matters."

Franklin came from a family with a devoutly Protestant tradition dating back to many years before their emigration to America—to the earliest years of the English Reformation, in fact. During the persecutions of Protestants in the reign of the Catholic Queen Mary (1553–1558) the Franklins courted real danger.

> This obscure family of ours [Franklin wrote in his *Autobiography*] was early in the Reformation, and continued Protestants through the reign of Queen Mary, when they were sometimes in danger of trouble on account of their zeal against popery. They had got an English Bible, and to conceal and secure it, it was fastened open with tapes under and within the cover of a joint-stool. When my great-great grandfather read it to his family, he turned up the joint-stool upon his knees, turning over the leaves then under the tapes. One of the children stood at the door to give notice if he saw the apparitor coming, who was an officer of the spiritual court. In that case the stool was turned down again upon its feet, when the Bible remained concealed under it as before. . . . The family continued all of the Church of England till about the end of Charles the Second's reign [1685], when some of the ministers that had been outed for non-conformity holding conventicles [secret Presbyterian services] in Northamptonshire, Benjamin and Josiah adhered to them, and so continued all their lives. . . .
>
> Josiah, my father, married young, and carried his wife with three children into New England, about 1682. The conventicles having been forbidden by law, and frequently disturbed, induced some considerable men of his acquaintance to remove to that country, and he was prevailed with to accompany them thither, where they expected to enjoy their mode of religion with freedom.

Franklin, then—like other key Founding Fathers such as John Jay of New York, who was of Huguenot stock—came from a family for which the bloody religious persecutions of the Reformation and the seventeenth century were indelible memories. The evils of religious strife were vivid and obvious to the Franklins, and were communicated to Benjamin at an early age. From his mother's family he received another example, this time not of the scourge of intolerance but of the grace of tolerance, in the benign person of his grandfather.

My mother . . . was Abiah Folger, daughter of Peter Folger, one of the first settlers of New England, of whom honorable mention is made by Cotton Mather. . . . I have heard that he wrote sundry small occasional pieces, but only one of them was printed, which I saw some many years since. It was written in 1675, in the home-spun taste of that time and people, and addressed to those then concerned in the government there. It was in favor of liberty of conscience, and in behalf of the Baptists, Quakers, and other sectaries that had been under persecution, ascribing the Indian wars, and other distresses that had befallen the country, to that persecution, as so many judgments of God to punish so heinous an offense, and exhorting a repeal of those uncharitable laws. The whole appeared to me as written with a good deal of decent plainness and manly freedom.

Franklin's father was a tallow-chandler with fourteen children of whom Benjamin, born in 1706, was the youngest boy. Money was very scarce, but Josiah Franklin respected education and realized that his youngest son had unusual intellectual gifts. Josiah was a staunch Presbyterian—a Calvinistic Puritan, in other words—and at first it was settled that the boy should become a minister; Josiah sent him to the Boston Latin School in preparation for divinity studies at Harvard. He withdrew him, however, after only a year. "My father, in the meantime," as Franklin recounted, "from a view of the expense of a college education, which having so large a family he could not well afford, and the mean living many so educated were afterwards able to obtain . . . altered his first intention, took me from the

grammar school, and sent me to a school for writing and arithmetic."
After a year at this second school, Franklin, now ten, was withdrawn
and put to work in the family tallow-chandler business, then, two
years later, apprenticed to his brother James, a printer.

One wonders whether financial considerations were Josiah's
only reasons for changing his mind about his son's future; some
have speculated that the young Franklin's skeptical, probing nature
was already evident and made him a very unlikely candidate for the
ministry. Certainly he displayed no special piety, then or ever: as the
historian Vernon Louis Parrington remarked of him, "the Calvinism in which he was bred left not the slightest trace upon him. He
was a free man who went his own way with imperturbable good will
and unbiased intelligence." Discussing his early reading, Franklin
derided contemporary works of theology—"My father's little library consisted chiefly of books in polemic divinity, most of which
I read, and have since regretted that, at a time when I had such a
thirst for knowledge, more proper books had not fallen in my way,
since it was now resolved I should not be a clergyman"—and re-
served his approval for authors who stressed good works rather
than doctrinal orthodoxy, specifically praising one "of Dr. Mather's,
called Essays to do Good, which perhaps gave me a turn of thinking that had an influence on some of the principal future events of
my life."

As a teenager Franklin continued his program of self-education,
devouring key texts of the British Enlightenment, of which John
Locke's *Essay Concerning Human Understanding*, the Earl of Shaftesbury's *Characteristics of Men, Manners, Opinions, and Times*, often referred to as "the deists' Bible," and the writings of the influential
deist Anthony Collins made the greatest impression: in the *Autobiography* Franklin recorded that his readings of Shaftesbury and Collins
had made him "a real doubter in many points of our religious doctrine." His parents disapproved of his unorthodox opinions, but the
boy had already moved beyond their narrower mental world.

My parents had early given me religious impressions, and brought me through my childhood piously in the Dissenting way. [That is, he was brought up as a Presbyterian, a Calvinist.] But I was scarce fifteen, when, after doubting by turns of several points, as I found them disputed in the different books I read, I began to doubt of Revelation itself. Some books against Deism fell into my hands. . . . It happened that they wrought an effect on me quite contrary to what was intended by them; for the arguments of the Deists, which were quoted to be refuted, appeared to me much stronger than the refutations; in short, I soon became a thorough Deist.

Franklin was not afraid to air his new opinions openly, and "my indiscreet disputations about religion," he later recalled, "began to make me pointed at with horror by many good people as an infidel or atheist." With the zeal of any convert, he became so dogmatic in his new creed that he eventually rose to a lofty plane of Panglossian complacency, concluding with Pope that "Whatever is, is right," and "from the attributes of God, his infinite wisdom, goodness and power . . . , that nothing could possibly be wrong in the world, and that vice and virtue were empty distinctions."

This was an absurd position from which he very soon backed down. "I began to suspect that this doctrine, tho' it might be true, was not very useful," he said, and he began, with the pragmatism that would define his entire life, to concoct a creed that put utility before theology, since he had concluded that theological truth was in any case unknowable and that to search for it was a waste of valuable time. "Revelation [including the Ten Commandments] had indeed no weight with me, as such," he admitted—a bold position entirely characteristic of Enlightenment intellectuals—"but I entertain'd an opinion that, though certain actions might not be bad *because* they were forbidden by it, or good *because* it commanded them, yet probably these actions might be forbidden *because* they were bad for us, or commanded

Franklin did not go so far in infidelity as Jefferson, who referred to Christianity as "our particular superstition," but he made it perfectly clear that he didn't think Christianity had any monopoly on the truth, and that it had violated all the good principles of civil society with its long history of intolerance. "If we look back into history for the character of the present sects in Christianity," he once wrote, "we shall find few that have not in their turns been persecutors, and complainers of persecution. The primitive Christians thought persecution extremely wrong in the Pagans, but practiced it on one another. The first Protestants of the Church of England blamed persecution in the Romish church, but practiced it upon the Puritans. These found it wrong in the Bishops, but fell into the same practice themselves both here [England] and in New England." It was Franklin's firmly held contention that "most sects in religion think themselves in possession of all truth, and that whenever others differ from them, it is so far error." He found a rare exception in the Dunkers, a Baptist denomination which, he discovered, was willing to change its dogma according to new discoveries and knowledge. "This modesty in a sect," he commented,

> is perhaps a singular instance in the history of mankind, every other sect supposing itself in possession of all truth, and that those who differ are so far in the wrong; like a man traveling in foggy weather, those at some distance before him on the road he sees wrapped up in the fog, as well as those behind him, and also the people in the fields on each side, but near him all appears clear, tho' in truth he is as much in the fog as any of them.

That non-Christian religious beliefs could be just as worthy of respect as—or, by extension, at least no more outlandish than—the Christian variety, his 1784 "Remarks concerning the Savages of North America" demonstrates:

A Swedish minister having assembled the chiefs of the
Susquehanna Indians, made a sermon to them, acquainting
them with the principal historical facts on which our religion is
founded, such as the fall of our first parents by eating an apple;
the coming of Christ to repair the mischief; his miracles and
sufferings, etc. When he had finished, an Indian orator stood
up to thank him. "What you have told us," said he, "is all very
good. It is indeed bad to eat apples. It is better to make them
all into cider. We are much obliged by your kindness in coming
so far to tell us those things which you have heard from your
mothers. In return, I will tell you some of those which we have
heard from ours. In the beginning, our fathers had only the
flesh of animals to subsist on; and if their hunting was
unsuccessful, they were starving. Two of our young hunters
having killed deer, made a fire in the woods to broil some parts
of it. When they were about to satisfy their hunger, they beheld
a beautiful young woman descend from the clouds, and seat
herself on that hill which you see yonder among the blue
mountains. They said to each other, it is a spirit that perhaps
has smelt our broiled venison and wishes to eat of it; let us
offer some to her. They presented her with the tongue; she was
pleased with the taste of it, and said, "Your kindness shall be
rewarded. Come to this place after thirteen moons, and you
shall find something that will be of a great benefit in
nourishing you and your children to the latest generations."
They did so and, to their surprise, found plants they had never
seen before; but which, from that ancient time, have been
constantly cultivated among us to our great advantage. Where
her right hand touched the ground they found maize; where
her left hand touched it they found kidney-beans." . . . The
good missionary, disgusted with this idle tale, said, "What I
delivered to you were sacred truths; but what you tell me is
mere fable, fiction, and falsehood." The Indian, offended,

replied, "My brother, it seems your friends have not done you justice in your education; they have not well instructed you in the rules of common civility. You saw that we, who understand and practice these rules, believed all your stories, why do you refuse to believe ours?"

Now there can be no doubt that this story is an example of religious relativism—written more than two hundred years before our so-called relativistic age began. The fact is that it displays an attitude that was the rule rather than the exception among the Enlightenment intellectuals who founded our country. A relativistic, anthropological vision of religious belief was much more characteristic of the Founding Fathers' ideas than the sort of monolithic Christian outlook asserted by today's fundamentalists.

When he wrote or spoke about matters of religion and dogma, Franklin tended to couch his messages in fables or humorous tales like the above. He had discovered very early what it takes most of us a lifetime to learn: that gentle persuasion is more effective than aggressive argumentation, a practice he referred to as disputatiousness. "A disputatious turn . . . is apt to become a very bad habit, making people often extremely disagreeable in company by the contradiction that is necessary to bring it into practice; and thence, besides souring and spoiling the conversation, is productive of disgusts and, perhaps, enmities where you have occasion for friendship." When he wished to influence someone's opinion he preferred the Socratic method: "I was charm'd with it, adopted it, dropt my abrupt contradiction and positive argumentation, and put on the humble inquirer and doubter. . . . [I retained] the habit of expressing myself in terms of modest diffidence; never using, when I advanced anything that may possibly be disputed, the words *certainly, undoubtedly,* or any others that give the air of positiveness to an opinion."

Religion, a topic on which passions run higher than any other, was naturally to be treated with special care, and Franklin was the first in a long line of American political manipulators far too savvy to underestimate the importance of at least paying lip service to religion, and at least pretending to respect the religious beliefs of others. To attack the foundations of popular religious belief, as he assured a friend who wanted to publish a skeptical manuscript, is inevitably fruitless and even counterproductive. ". . . [T]hough your Reasonings are subtile, and may prevail with some Readers, you will not succeed so as to change the general Sentiments of Mankind on that Subject," he insisted, "and the Consequence of printing this Piece will be, a great deal of Odium drawn upon yourself, Mischief to you, and no Benefit to others. He that spits against the Wind, spits in his own Face."

But by using pseudonyms and sugarcoating his ideas with humor, Franklin was able to get away with a good deal. At a mere sixteen years of age, for instance, the precocious Franklin was attacking the habit, widespread then as now, of co-opting religious piety in the service of political skullduggery. These comments appeared in a series of letters to his brother James's newspaper, *The New England Courant*, in which Franklin adopted the persona of a middle-aged woman, "Silence Dogood":

> It has been for some Time a Question with me, Whether a Common-wealth suffers more by hypocritical Pretenders to Religion, or by the openly Profane? But some late thoughts of this Nature, have inclined me to think, that the Hypocrite is the most dangerous Person of the Two, especially if he sustains a post in the Governement, and we consider his Conduct as it regards the Publick. . . .
>
> A man compounded of Law and Gospel, is able to cheat a whole country with his Religion, and then destroy them under *Colour of Law*.

In 1729 Franklin started *The Pennsylvania Gazette*, which was to become the leading newspaper in the colony. Two imaginary dialogues he printed in it in 1730 say much about his moral ideas as they were developing: "A Dialogue Between Philocles and Horatio, Meeting Accidentally in the Fields, Concerning Virtue and Pleasure" (1730), proving that "a vicious man could not properly be called a man of sense," and "A Second Dialogue Between Philocles and Horatio, Concerning Virtue and Pleasure," which showed that "virtue was not secure till its practice became a habitude, and was free from the opposition of contrary inclinations." These dialogues and their conclusions owe a good deal less to the wisdom and ethos of the Gospels than they do to the philosophy of Aristotle, whose *Nichomachean Ethics* stresses the idea that to *become* virtuous one must develop the *habit* of performing virtuous acts. Franklin, like Washington and Jefferson, really owed more of his ethical and moral code to the classical writers, and in particular to the Stoics and Epicureans, than he did to the tenets of Christianity.

One incident in particular permanently discouraged Franklin from involving himself in religious controversy of any description: the so-called Hemphill affair of 1734. The Reverend Samuel Hemphill delivered a series of sermons in Philadelphia that stressed good works over faith and salvation; Franklin, who thoroughly approved of the message, had helped him write some of these and supported Hemphill in the pages of *The Pennsylvania Gazette* when he was attacked by an old-style Calvinist, the Reverend Jedediah Andrews (the same minister whose "dry, uninteresting and unedifying" sermons had "disgusted" him). Eventually Hemphill was suspended by the Presbyterian synod; Franklin was disgusted anew and thenceforth severed all association with the church.

As the Franklin biographer A. O. Aldridge has said, "Both before and after the Hemphill affair, Franklin used the *Gazette* as an organ of concealed deism and open latitudinarianism." In 1739, though, he had a brief—very brief—flirtation with evangelical Christianity in the person of the extraordinarily charismatic George Whitefield, who arrived in Philadelphia that year on his triumphal tour of the American colonies. His visit kicked off what we now call "The Great Awakening," an evangelical movement that swept the American colonies in the 1740s. "His eloquence had a wonderful power over the hearts and purses of his hearers," Franklin later wrote, "of which I myself was an instance."

Whitefield was collecting money for an orphanage he proposed to build in the colony of Georgia. Franklin, by then a leading citizen of Philadelphia, was naturally approached as a potential donor, but while he approved of the general idea of the orphanage, he disagreed with Whitefield on various particulars and therefore declined to contribute. However,

> I happened soon after to attend one of his sermons, in the course of which I perceived he intended to finish with a collection, and I silently resolved he should get nothing from me. I had in my pocket a handful of copper money, three or four silver dollars, and five pistoles in gold. As he proceeded I began to soften, and concluded to give the coppers. Another stroke of his oratory made me asham'd of that, and determin'd me to give the silver; and he finish'd so admirably, that I empty'd my pocket wholly into the collector's dish, gold and all.

Knowing what a hard nut he himself had been to crack, Franklin was full of admiration for Whitefield's oratorical powers. These appealed, finally, not to his religious impulses but to his scientific ones, and with typical Enlightenment skepticism he determined to find out just how Whitefield had pulled off the trick: there must be a scientific explanation for his success in the pulpit.

> He had a loud and clear voice, and articulated his words and sentences so perfectly, that he might be heard and understood at a great distance, especially as his auditories, however numerous, observ'd the most exact silence. He preach'd one evening from the top of the Court-house steps, which are in

the middle of Market-street, and on the west side of Second-
street, which crosses it at right angles. Both streets were fill'd
with his hearers to a considerable distance. Being among the
hindmost in Market-street, I had the curiosity to learn how far
back he could be heard, by retiring backwards down the street
towards the river; and I found his voice distinct till I came near
Front-street, when some noise in that street obscur'd it.
Imagining then a semi-circle, of which my distance should be
the radius, and that it were fill'd with auditors, to each of
whom I allow'd two square feet, I computed that he might well
be heard by more than thirty thousand. This reconciled me to
the newspaper accounts of his having preach'd to twenty-five
thousand people in the fields, and to the antient histories of
generals haranguing whole armies, of which I had sometimes
doubted.

By hearing him often, I came to distinguish easily between
sermons newly compos'd, and those which he had often
preach'd in the course of his travels. His delivery of the latter
was so improv'd by frequent repetitions that every accent,
every emphasis, every modulation of voice, was so perfectly
well turn'd and well plac'd, that, without being interested in the
subject, one could not help being pleas'd with the discourse; a
pleasure of much the same kind with that receiv'd from an
excellent piece of musick. [So much, it seems, for divine
inspiration.] This is an advantage itinerant preachers have over
those who are stationary, as the latter can not well improve their
delivery of a sermon by so many rehearsals.

. . . I am of opinion if he had never written any thing, he
would have left behind him a much more numerous and
important sect, and his reputation might in that case have been
still growing, even after his death, as there might be nothing of
his writing on which to found a censure and give him a lower
character, his proselytes would be left at liberty to feign for him

as great a variety of excellences as their enthusiastic admiration might wish him to have possessed.

Nothing could better illustrate Franklin's consummately empiricist attitude to life. Where other listeners would have found Whitefield's superb oratory evidence of divine inspiration, Franklin recognized it as the result of long and painstaking practice. He pointed out, too, the fleeting and unreliable nature of auditory impressions when he remarked that the actual content of Whitefield's sermons, as indicated in his writings, was not equal in quality to the rhetorical magnificence of his performance.

Whitefield was pained by Franklin's incorrigible paganism, but like everyone else he succumbed to his charm, and the two remained friends for years. Whitefield never gave up in his attempt to lead the great man of science to Jesus. "I do not despair of your seeing the reasonableness of Christianity," he wrote him in 1740. "Apply to GOD; be willing to do the divine will, and you shall know it." And again twelve years later: "[A]s you have made a pretty considerable progress in the mysteries of electricity, I would now humbly recommend to your diligent unprejudiced pursuit and study the mystery of the new-birth. . . ." But all in vain: as Franklin remarked in his *Autobiography*, Whitefield "us'd indeed sometimes to pray for my Conversion, but never had the satisfaction of believing that his prayers were heard." Characteristic of their relationship was Franklin's suggestion that the minister should stay at his house on an upcoming visit to Philadelphia. "He reply'd, that if I made that kind offer for Christ's sake, I should not miss of a reward. And I returned, *"Don't let me be mistaken; it was not for Christ's sake, but for your sake."*

Another longtime friend who despaired of Franklin's irreligion was the famous scientist Dr. Joseph Priestley, the discoverer of oxygen and a notorious and outspoken deist. His worries over Franklin's soul might seem rather suprising, since Priestley's own faith was a

Unitarianism of the broadest possible type; in fact he was often derided as an infidel and had been hounded out of his native England
for opinions most Englishmen considered heretical. "It is much to
be lamented," Priestley wrote in his autobiography, "that a man of
Franklin's general good character and great influence should have
been an unbeliever in Christianity, and also have done as much as he
did to make others unbelievers."

Franklin was a great diplomat—indeed one of the greatest diplo-
mats of all time, on a par with Metternich and Talleyrand, and he
was almost single-handedly responsible for obtaining and keeping
the French aid that enabled the Americans to win their independence. The scope of his diplomatic gifts can be seen in the wide variety of friendships he managed to maintain simultaneously, from
supposed infidels like Priestley and Thomas Paine, to real ones like
the French *philosophes* D'Holbach and Condorcet, to devout Christians like Whitefield.

As president of the Pennsylvania Constitutional Convention in
charge of creating a constitution for the new state, Franklin declared
his dislike of religious tests—that is, the practice of requiring public
officeholders to profess a formal adherence to an established church.
These were invented, he believed, "not so much to secure religion as
the emoluments of it [that is, the financial support of churchmen].
When a religion is good, I conceive that it will support itself; and
when it does not support itself, and God does not take care to support it, so that its professors are obliged to call for help of the civil
power, 'tis a sign, I apprehend, of its being a bad one." He vehe-
mently but fruitlessly opposed the Convention's decision to require
all voters and officeholders to declare a belief in God and in the divine authority of the Old and New Testaments.

> I agreed with you [he wrote Dr. Priestley] in sentiments
> concerning the Old Testament, and thought the clause in our
> [Pennsylvania] Constitution, which required the members of

the Assembly to declare their belief that the whole of it was given by divine inspiration, had better have been omitted. That I had opposed the clause; but being overpowered by numbers, and fearing more in future might be grafted on it, I prevailed to have the additional clause, "that no further or more extended profession of faith should ever be exacted." I observed to you, too, that the evil of it was the less, as no inhabitant, nor any officer of government, except the members of Assembly, was obliged to make the declaration.

When Franklin assumed the office of governor of Pennsylvania in 1786, he and the state assembly repealed the offensive law so "as to confer equal privileges upon every citizen of the state"—Christian and non-Christian alike.

Franklin's most famous act *in favor of* religion came at the Constitutional Convention of the United States in 1787, when he moved that the daily sessions, which had heretofore been decidedly acrimonious, be opened with a prayer. The words of his motion were specifically nondenominational, referring to God, the Father of Lights, and Providence interchangeably; the name of Jesus Christ was certainly not mentioned. It was an elegant and propitiatory gesture from a man who respected what he saw as the essence of religion—respect for the Maker, and humility respecting one's own infinitesimal place within Creation—rather than its trappings. The delegates gave the issue a desultory debate, but there seemed too many objections against such a scheme: the choice of any specific minister to lead the prayers would unfairly favor that minister's denomination over others, there were no extra funds to pay such a person, and so forth. The matter was dropped quickly and without even the formality of a vote. As Franklin noted dryly in his journal, "The Convention, except three or four persons, thought prayer unnecessary."

In the last year of Franklin's life, Ezra Stiles, the president of Yale, asked the great man for a confidential summary of his religious beliefs. Franklin's response, written just six weeks before his death at the age of eighty-four, was honest and should be taken at face value.

> Here is my creed. I believe in one God, Creator of the universe. That he governs it by his providence. That he ought to be worshipped. That the most acceptable service we render to him is doing good to his other children. That the soul of Man is immortal, and will be treated with justice in another life respecting its conduct in this. These I take to be the fundamental points in all sound religion, and I regard them as you do in whatever sect I meet with them.
>
> As for Jesus of Nazareth, my opinion of whom you particularly desire, I think his system of morals and his religion, as he left them to us, the best the world ever saw or is likely to see; but I apprehend it has received various corrupting changes, and I have, with most of the present dissenters in England, some doubts as to his divinity; though it is a question that I do not dogmatize upon, having never studied it, and think it needless to busy myself with now, when I expect soon an opportunity of knowing the truth with less trouble. I see no harm, however, in its being believed, if that belief has the good consequence, as it probably has, of making his doctrines more respected and better observed, especially as I do not perceive that the Supreme takes it amiss, by distinguishing the unbelievers in his government of the world with any particular marks of his displeasure.

The question of whether or not Christ was the son of God appeared not only unanswerable to Franklin but finally a matter of indifference. But as a politician and diplomat he had a reputation to protect and countless professional and personal ties to maintain; it would have done him no good to disavow a belief in the tenets of Christianity. Therefore he urged Stiles to respect his privacy and under no account to share his opinions, proffered in confidence, with anyone else.

> I confide, that you will not expose me to criticism and censure by publishing any part of this communication to you. I have ever let others enjoy their religious sentiments without reflecting on them for those that appeared unsupportable and even absurd. All sects here [in Philadelphia], and we have a great variety, have experienced my good will in assisting them with subscriptions for building their new places of worship; and, as I have never opposed any of their doctrines, I hope to go out of the world in peace with them all.

CHAPTER TWO

Washington

훚 GEORGE WASHINGTON was always a bit of a mystery man, maintaining an impeccably formal front while keeping his private thoughts to himself. Upon the question of his religious beliefs he was more reticent than on any other: during his lifetime and long after his death, even close associates and friends were not sure just what these amounted to. Here is Thomas Jefferson's journal entry, dated eighteen years after Washington's death, in which he speculates whether or not the great man had been a Christian:

> Doctor [Benjamin] Rush tells me that he had it from Asa Green [the Reverend Ashbel Green, chaplain to Congress during Washington's administration] that when the clergy addressed General Washington on his departure from the Government, it was observed in their consultation, that he had never, on any occasion, said a word to the public which showed a belief in the Christian religion, and they thought they should so pen their address, as to force him at length to declare publicly whether he was a Christian or not. They did so.
>
> However, he observed, the old fox was too cunning for them. He answered every article of their address particularly

except that, which he passed over without notice. Rush observes, he never did say a word on the subject in any of his public papers, except in his valedictory letter to the Governors of the States, when he resigned his commission in the army, wherein he speaks of the "benign influence of the Christian religion." I know that Gouverneur Morris, who pretended [i.e., claimed] to be in his secrets and believed himself to be so, has often told me that General Washington believed no more in that system than he himself did.

Washington's famous gift of silence, his ability to completely ignore any unpleasant questions and go on his way without committing himself on dangerous subjects, had long been a subject of remark and envy among his peers. In 1807 Benjamin Rush wrote to John Adams that "upon the subject of [Washington's] taciturnity, Mr. Liston [the British minister in America] gave me the following anecdote: 'That he was the only person he had ever known (and he had conversed with several crowned heads, and many of the first nobility in Europe) who made *no reply* of any kind to a question that he did not choose to answer.'" Adams, who had spent eight years as Washington's vice president, heartily concurred. "Washington! Franklin! Jefferson! Eternal silence! impenetrable secrecy! deep cunning! These are the talents and virtues which are triumphant in these days." No subject has ever been more dangerous to politicians than religion, as Washington was well aware. His opinions on the subject mystified even members of the Anglican clergy who knew him well: Bishop William White of Philadelphia, who presided at one of the two churches Washington attended in that city while president, wrote that he "knew no man who seemed so carefully to guard against the discoursing of himself or of his acts, or of anything pertaining to him"; the Reverend Samuel Miller commented that Washington displayed an "unusual but uniform reticence on the subject of religion."

There are very real doubts as to whether Washington was a Christian or even whether he was a believer at all. At most he was what his biographer Joseph Ellis has called "a lukewarm Episcopalian." He believed, or professed to believe, that religion improves morals, but religion seems to have played a remarkably small role in his own life. He seems to have modeled his character far more closely on classical ideals than on Christian ones.

But Washington, through the unique role he played in the American fight for independence and the establishment of the republic, and the actorly skill with which he performed it, became *the* First Citizen in United States history, the emblematic American, the poster boy for everything Americans like to think they stand for. In a Christian country, then, how could the greatest American not be a great Christian too? Any alternative has always been very frightening to those Americans who believe public morality to be contingent upon religious faith. Washington's death on December 14, 1799, coincided exactly with the close of the skeptical eighteenth century and the beginning of the pious nineteenth: the Second Great Awakening, from which the country has never quite recovered, had begun to sweep the nation. The Greatest American could not be allowed to rest in peace as what he had been, an undogmatic, perhaps skeptical Enlightenment gentleman: he must be remade in the image of the nineteenth-century true believer. So began the creation of the priggish George Washington ("I cannot tell a lie") we all learned about as children. It is a false and cartoonish portrait.

Washington was, as modern promoters of the evangelical agenda constantly remind us, a member of the Episcopal church throughout his life, and served as a vestryman in the Truro Parish of his native Virginia. Well, yes, of course; it was what the pillars of the Virginia establishment did throughout the eighteenth, nineteenth, and even twentieth centuries. From 1759, when this obscure member of the Virginia gentry married Martha Dandrige Custis, the richest widow in the Tidewater, Washington was a large-scale grandee whose posi-

tion absolutely demanded that he take his part in the rites and rituals of the Episcopal church, the established church in the colony of
Virginia. For him to have done otherwise would have been eccentric
in the extreme, and it was not in Washington's nature ever to wish to
seem eccentric. Even the openly anti-Christian Jefferson, and
George Wythe, another freethinking Founding Father, served as
vestrymen, as befitted their families' important positions within the
social structure of the Old Dominion. Moreover the vestry at that
time also functioned as the county court, and landowners had to control it if they wished to control their own extensive holdings and interests. Virginia's upper class, as the religious historian Frank Lambert has stressed, saw the Anglican church "more as an instrument
of social control than as a vehicle of personal salvation," and the
church hierarchy reflected and reinforced the prevailing social establishment. Another historian, H. J. Eckenrode, has bluntly characterized the typical Anglican twelve-man vestry as "a local oligarchy
of hard-fisted and often ignorant squires, who were interested in
keeping expenses down."

Nothing in what we know of Washington's tenure as a vestryman belies this judgment. In the thirty-seven fat volumes that make
up the bicentennial edition of Washington's papers there are only
four mentions of his vestry responsibilities, each one simply a com-
plaint about his having paid more than he felt he owed for some expense or other. The following, from 1796, is typical: "It is hardly possible it can be three years since I subscribed to the Salary of Mr.
Davis [the Reverend Thomas Davis of Christ Church, Alexandria],
how then can there be two years due when one has been paid? Surely
it was not the terms of the subscription to pay ten pounds at the beginning, and ten pounds at the end of the first year. . . . I am always
willing to pay what I owe, but *never* that which I *do not* owe." Washington's eventual resignation from the vestry, in 1784, was exceedingly abrupt: "It is not convenient for me to be at Colchester tomor-
row, and as I shall no longer act as a vestryman, the sooner my place

is filled with another the better. This letter, or something more formal if required, may evidence my resignation, and authorize a new choice."

Washington was very much a product of the planter society of the Tidewater and the ultimate exemplar of its mores at their very best. It is therefore necessary for the reader to understand those mores. Here are two historians' descriptions of the planter elite during the colonial period.

> No one can pretend that [the planter oligarchy's] piety was always remarkable, but, like the best of the English gentry, they looked upon religion as necessary to decent and respectable living and as essential to a well-ordered state. Since the members of the ruling class, almost without exception, were orthodox Anglicans, they labored to maintain conformity in the colony. The control of the church was in the hands of the great planters, who served as vestry men and church wardens and took a serious view of their duties. (From *The First Gentlemen of Virginia* by Louis B. Wright)

> [Planter] society seemed to visitors from the North remarkably easygoing and even frivolous. In Williamsburg and Annapolis, the two tiny capitals, cards, racing, and the theater were normal parts of the legislative season. Parsons seldom opposed these pursuits and sometimes took cordial part in them. In the correspondence of young men of the dominant class, a light tone was conventional, with much sighing over the cruelty of the fair Belinda or Phyllis and a complete absence of religious references. . . . Planters were seldom interested in theological dispute or mystical contemplation. What they wanted was a decent, orderly religion which would remind everybody of his position, his duties, and his limitations. (From *The Enlightenment in America* by Henry F. May)

George Washington's personal piety was no more remarkable than that of his less famous peers. He paid little attention to the Sabbath or any other outward manifestations of religiosity. We have various eyewitness accounts of life at Mount Vernon which do not much feature religious observance. Ona Judge Staines, for instance, a former Washington slave, remarked when she was interviewed in old age that "the stories of Washington's piety and prayers, so far as she ever saw or heard while she was his slave, have no foundation. Card-playing and wine-drinking were the business at his parties, and he had more of such company Sundays than on any other day." A visiting military officer from France was rather surprised when he dined with Washington, expecting this *paterfamilias* to say grace in what he had been led to believe was the American fashion. "The first time that I dined with him there was no clergyman and I did not perceive that he made this prayer, yet I remember that on taking his place at the table, he made a gesture and said a word, which I took for a piece of politeness, and which was perhaps a religious action. In this case his prayer must have been short; the clergyman made use of more forms. We remained a very long time at the table. They drank 12 or 15 healths with Madeira wine. In the course of the meal beer was served and grum, rum mixed with water."

Washington was not an avid churchgoer by any standards: his journals indicate that he attended church no more than twelve times a year or so. During his presidency his attendance at divine service was much more regular, as might be expected, but during the last three years of his life he seems to have attended church only three times. Significantly—and in the absence of any personal statements from Washington himself concerning his religious beliefs or lack of such, we have to treat such evidence as significant—he made it a point not to take communion, though his wife always did so. He would leave the church well ahead of Martha, thus requiring the coachman to make two trips back to the Washington home. We have ample authority for this fact. In 1835, for instance, a Colonel Mercer

wrote an inquiring letter to Bishop White. "I have a desire, my dear
Sir, to know whether Gen. Washington was a communicant of the
Protestant Episcopal church. . . . No authority can be so authentic
and complete as yours on this point." Bishop White's response was
the following: "Dear Sir: In regard to the subject of your inquiry,
truth requires me to say that Gen. Washington never received the
communion in the churches of which I am the parochial minister.
Mrs. Washington was an habitual communicant. . . . I have been
written to by many on that point, and have been obliged to answer
them as I now do you."

In his eight years as president, Washington attended both
White's church and another church in Philadelphia under the authority of the Reverend James Abercrombie. Here is Abercrombie's
recollection of Washington, as recounted by the Reverend William
B. Sprague in his *Annals of the American Pulpit*:

> One incident in Dr. Abercrombie's experience as a clergyman,
> in connection with the Father of his Country, is especially
> worthy of record; and the following account of it was given by
> the Doctor himself, in a letter to a friend, in 1831 shortly after
> there had been some public allusion to it: "With respect to the
> inquiry you make I can only state the following fact; that, as
> pastor of the Episcopal church, observing that, on sacramental
> Sundays, Gen. Washington, immediately after the desk and
> pulpit services, went out with the greater part of the
> congregation—always leaving Mrs. Washington with the other
> communicants—she invariably being one—I considered it my
> duty in a sermon on Public Worship, to state the unhappy
> tendency of example, particularly of those in elevated stations
> who uniformly turned their backs upon the celebration of the
> Lord's Supper. I acknowledge the remark was intended for the
> President; and as such he received it. A few days after, in
> conversation with, I believe, a senator of the United States, he

told me he had dined the day before with the President, who in the course of conversation at table said that on the preceding Sunday he had received a very just reproof from the pulpit for always leaving the church before the administration of the sacrament; that he honored the preacher for his integrity and candor; that he had never sufficiently considered the influence of his example, and that he would not again give cause for the repetition of the reproof; and that, as he had never been a communicant, were he to become one then it would be imputed to an ostentatious display of religious zeal arising altogether from his elevated station. Accordingly, he never afterwards came on the morning of sacramental Sunday, though at other times he was a constant attendant in the morning.

Whatever Washington's refusal to take communion might say about his beliefs or lack thereof, it proves that he was the very opposite of the sort of religious hypocrite excoriated by Benjamin Franklin: he would have scorned to mix law and gospel. His unwillingness to provide the populace with "an ostentatious display of religious zeal" says a great deal not so much about his religion as about his personal integrity, and contrasts sharply with the example of some of his successors.

In death Washington was no more zealous than he had been in life. At the time of his death in 1799 it was the custom of believing Christians to attempt to have a man of God present at their deathbeds, and to join this minister in prayer if possible. Washington requested no such supernatural aid in his final hours, though he was well aware that he was dying. His last act on earth, in fact, was to take his own pulse, the consummate Enlightenment gesture: as his biographer Joseph Ellis has written, "there were no ministers in the room, no prayers uttered, no Christian rituals offering the solace of everlasting life." Ellis points out, though, that "the inevitable renderings of Washington's death by nineteenth-century artists often added religious symbols to the scene, frequently depicting his body ascending into heaven surrounded by a chorus of angels. The historical evidence suggests that Washington did not think much about heaven or angels; the only place he knew his body was going was into the ground, and as for his soul, its ultimate location was unknowable. He died as a Roman Stoic rather than a Christian saint."

Bishop White, along with many others, suspected that Washington was a deist, unconvinced of biblical revelation or Christ's divinity. "His behavior [in church] was always serious and attentive, but as your letter seems to intend an inquiry on the point of kneeling during the service, I owe it to the truth to declare that I never saw him in the said attitude," he wrote to one curious acquaintance; ". . . Although I was often in company with this great man, and had the honor of dining often at this table, I never heard anything from him which could manifest his opinions on the subject of religion." In a subsequent letter to the same correspondent, White added, "I do not believe that any degree of recollection will bring to my mind any fact which would prove General Washington to have been a believer in the Christian revelation further than as may be hoped from his constant attendance upon Christian worship, in connection with the general reserve of his character." The Reverend Dr. Bird Wilson, an Episcopal minister in Albany, New York, wrote in 1831 that Washington "was esteemed by the whole world as a great and good man; but he was not a professing Christian." Abercrombie had responded to Wilson's questioning on the subject briefly but resoundingly: "Sir, Washington was a Deist."

What exactly were Washington's religious beliefs? The evidence of his personal letters and papers would seem to point away from the Christian faith in the direction of the deist or even Stoic beliefs. General A. W. Greely, whose extensive study of the first president resulted in an article called "Washington's Domestic and Religious

Life," concluded that "the effort to depict Washington as very devout from his childhood, as a strict Sabbatarian, and as in intimate spiritual communication with the church is practically contradicted by his own letters." In those letters, Greely pointed out, "even those of consolation, there appears almost nothing to indicate his spiritual frame of mind." Greely found it especially striking that "in several thousand letters the name of Jesus Christ never appears, and it is notably absent from his last will."

Greely was correct: the name of Jesus is conspicuous by its absence. Washington's letters to his wife were destroyed after his death, so we are denied any clue to his beliefs that might have been contained in them, but the rest of his very voluminous correspondence, both intimate and official, fails to mention a savior or redeemer. In a longish lifetime—sixty-seven years—there are only a couple of passing references to Christianity: the aforementioned reference to the benign influence of the Christian religion, and a brief word on the Indian tribes, expressing his official approval of their conversion. Jesus himself is not mentioned anywhere in Washington's correspondence. In marked contrast with Jefferson, Franklin, Adams, and even the scandalous Thomas Paine, he did not even make any reference to Jesus as a great philosopher or moralist. Stranger yet, when the Congress used the name of Jesus Christ in their occasional calls for days of thanksgiving, Washington would modify the wording of these proclamations so as to avoid using the name. Nor is there any evidence in his writings that he entertained any expectation of eternal life, an essential Christian tenet. All this can hardly have been an oversight. Washington was a methodical, meticulous man. He was also scrupulously honest, and on occasions where he did not feel honesty to be the best policy he kept his mouth diplomatically shut, as Jefferson, Adams, and Rush had all remarked.

It is interesting to note that the occasional letters of advice Washington penned to various stepchildren and nephews contained no injunctions whatsoever on religious observance and indeed no mention of religion at all, though he proffered considerable advice on moral and ethical subjects. Letters from the 1780s and 1790s to Bushrod Washington, George Steptoe Washington, and Harriot Washington are particularly extensive and of great interest to those interested in Washington's practical philosophy.

The perusal of Washington's writings, speeches, and personal papers shows a man with a practical code of ethics rather than any sort of mystical faith, Christian or otherwise. He eschewed the loaded word "God" whenever possible, opting instead for some nondenominational moniker like Superintending Power, Great Ruler of Events, Higher Cause, Grand Architect of the Universe—all of which terms he used more or less interchangeably with Providence, a force hardly distinguishable from the pagan idea of "Fortuna." A couple of examples of his writing will clearly illustrate this way of thinking. First, from a letter to his friend Bryan Fairfax: "The determinations of Providence are all ways wise; often inscrutable, and though its decrees appear to bear hard upon us at times is nevertheless meant for gracious purposes; in this light I cannot help viewing your latest disappointment. . . ." And, in a public statement: "In what way they will terminate, is known only to the great ruler of events; and confiding in his wisdom and goodness, we may safely trust the issue to him, without perplexing ourselves to seek for that, which is beyond human ken; only taking care to perform the parts assigned us, in a way that reason and our own consciences approve of."

This philosophy impresses one as far more Stoic than Christian, as a number of historians have observed. An educated man of the eighteenth century would have been conversant with, and favorably disposed toward, the Stoic ethos. Unlike the other key founding fathers discussed in this book, Washington was not an intellectual and seems to have had no special interest in religion as an abstract, anthropological study (Jefferson and Adams were passionately interested in this subject, to which they devoted much of their mental energy far into old age); he was a man of action, with a practical ethos tailored to the demands of his extraordinary life. But he was also a well-read gentleman of fairly broad, liberal interests, familiar with ancient history and the classics, who had been brought up in a social climate entirely different from the fervent Calvinism of New England.

> The virtues of the [Virginia] gentleman owed more to Aristotle than to Christian writings, though, from the middle of the seventeenth century onward, the religious note grew stronger. Fortitude, temperance, prudence, and justice were the four cardinal virtues that Aristotle and succeeding classical writers laid down as fundamental to the gentleman. . . . Piety was often commended in the conduct books, even assumed in some degree, for the gentleman must set an example of religious observance to lesser folk. The aim most frequently recommended was to seek Aristotle's golden mean between extremes—a goal which led to moderation in everything, including religion. (From *The First Gentlemen of Virginia* by Louis B. Wright)

An easy latitudinarianism, the idealization of the Aristotelian mean, or *mediocritas*, a somewhat snobbish contempt for showy zeal in religious matters, a benign tolerance for skepticism and deism: all these qualities set the Virginia gentleman apart from his more publicly pious brethren in New England. The following quotation from the *Meditations* of the second-century Stoic emperor Marcus Aurelius (in a rather free translation by Gregory Hays) is far, far more pertinent to Washington's personal code of conduct than anything to be found in either the Old or New Testaments.

> How to act:
> Never under compulsion, out of selfishness, without
>   forethought, with misgivings.
> Don't gussy up your thoughts.

No surplus words or unnecessary actions.

Let the spirit in you represent a man, an adult, a citizen, a
    Roman, a ruler. Taking up his post like a soldier and
    patiently awaiting his recall from life. Needing no oath or
    witness.

Cheerfulness. Without requiring other people's help. Or
    serenity supplied by others.

John Adams, always jealous of Washington's apparently effort-
less dignity and authority and his unrivaled status as a Great Man,
speculated cynically with his friend Benjamin Rush about just how
Washington had arrived at his magnificent personality.

I have sometimes amused myself with inquiring where
Washington got his system. Was it the natural growth of his
own great genius? Had there been any examples of it in
Virginia? Instances enough might have been found in history
of excellent hypocrites, whose concealments, dissimulations,
and simulations had deceived the world for a time; and some
great examples of real disinterestedness, which produced the
noblest efforts and have always been acknowledged. But you
know that our beloved Washington was but very superficially
read in history of any age, nation, or country. [At least by
Adams's own superhuman standards.] Where then did he
obtain his instruction? I tell you what I conjecture.

Rollin's *Ancient History*,* you know is very generally
diffused through this country because it has been and is in
England. The reading of most of our men of letters extends
little further than this work and Prideaux's *Connections of the
Old and New Testaments*. From Rollin I suspect Washington
drew his wisdom, in a great measure. In the third chapter of

---

*Charles Rollin, *Ancient History* (Paris, 1730–1738), a popular history considered
very lightweight by hard-hitting intellectuals like Adams.

the third book . . . there are in the character of Dejoces several strokes which are very curious as they resemble the politics of so many of our countrymen, though the whole character taken together is far inferior in purity and magnanimity to that of Washington. "He retired from public business, pretending to be over fatigued with the multitudes of people that resorted to him." "His own domestic affairs would not allow him to attend those of other people" &c. . . .

There is nothing certainly nobler or greater than to see a private person eminent for his merit and virtue and fitted by his excellent talents for the highest employments, and yet through inclination and modesty preferring a life of obscurity and retirement; than to see such a man sincerely refuse the offer made to him of reigning over a whole nation, and at last consent to undergo the toil of government, upon no other motive than that of being serviceable to his fellow citizens. His first disposition, by which he declares that he is acquainted with the duties and consequently the dangers annexed to a sovereign power, shows him to have a soul more elevated and great than greatness itself, or, to speak more justly, a soul superior to all ambition. . . . But when he generously sacrifices his own quiet and satisfaction to the welfare and tranquility of the public, it is plain he understands what that sovereign power has in it, really good or truly valuable; which is that it puts a man in a condition of becoming the defender of his country, of procuring it many advantages, and of redressing various evils . . . and he comforts himself for the cares and troubles to which he is exposed by the prospect of the many benefits resulting from them to the public. Such a governor was Numa at Rome, and such have been some other emperors, whom the people have constrained to accept the supreme power. . . .

Adams certainly had a point: Rollin might easily have been describing Washington himself.

In spite of—or perhaps *because* of—his indifference to the mere trappings of religion, Washington proved a great friend to religious liberty. He described his own religious tenets as "few and simple" and himself as "no bigot to any mode of worship," and he strongly endorsed the Lockean proposition that, in Washington's own words, "While men perform their social duties faithfully, they do all that society or the state can with propriety demand or expect; and remain responsible to their Maker for the religion, or modes of faith, which they may prefer or profess." The various addresses he gave during the course of his presidency to churches, synagogues, and religious groups all strike a similar note, and strike it with real conviction. For instance:

> We have abundant reason to rejoice that in this Land the light of truth and reason has triumphed over the power of bigotry and superstition. . . . In this enlightened Age and in this Land of equal liberty it is our boast, that a man's religious tenets will not forfeit the protection of the Laws, nor deprive him of the right of attaining and holding the highest Offices that are known in the United States. (From a letter to the members of the New Church in Baltimore, January 27, 1793)

> The Citizens of the United States of America have a right to applaud themselves for having given to mankind examples of an enlarged and liberal policy: a policy worthy of imitation. . . . It is now no more that toleration is spoken of, as if it was by the indulgence of one class of people, that another enjoyed the free exercise of their inherent natural rights. For happily the Government of the United States, which gives to bigotry no sanction, to persecution no assistance, requires only that they who live under its protection should demean themselves as good citizens, in giving it on all occasions their effectual support. (From a letter to the congregation of the Touro Synagogue in Newport, Rhode Island, August 18, 1790)

As mankind becomes more liberal, they will be more apt to allow, that all those who conduct themselves as worthy members of the community are equally entitled to the protection of civil government. I hope ever to see America among the foremost nations in examples of justice and liberality. (From the Reply to a Congratulatory Address by a Committee of Roman Catholics Waiting Upon the President, March 15, 1790)

Government being, among other purposes, instituted to protect the persons and consciences of men from oppression, it certainly is the duty of rulers, not only to abstain from it themselves, but according to their stations, to prevent it in others. (From the Reply to an Address Sent by the Religious Society Called Quakers, September 28, 1789)

I am persuaded, you will permit me to observe, that the path of true piety is so plain as to require but little political direction. To this consideration we ought to ascribe the absence of any regulation, respecting religion, from the Magna Charta of our country. (From a letter to the ministers and elders representing the Massachusetts and New Hampshire Churches which compose the First Presbytery of Eastward, Newburyport, October 28, 1789)

I now send my best wishes to the Cherokees, and pray the Great Spirit to preserve them. (From an Address to the Cherokee Nation, August 29, 1796)

The question of how, or indeed whether, religion influences morality has been long and hotly debated. (Jefferson, who believed the moral sense to be an inborn human trait, sometimes went so far as to question whether religion had any practical utility at all: "If we did a good act merely from the love of God and a belief that it is pleasing to Him," he pondered, "whence arises the morality of the

Atheist? It is idle to say, as some do, that no such being exists.")
Washington, more conventional, plumped for the conventional idea
that religion, at least among the lower orders, is necessary not only
for personal morality but for the well-being of the state—though he
did not seem to care what form that religion might take. As a member of a conventional ruling class, he believed that religion would
uphold the social order; as a politician of the greatest skill, he had
learned that it would also uphold the political one.

As commander-in-chief during the Revolutionary War, Washington had often issued orders that the troops should attend religious
service in the interest of military discipline, cohesion, and *esprit de
corps*. "The Commander in chief thinks it a duty to declare the reg-
ularity and decorum with which divine service is now performed
every Sunday, will reflect great credit on the army in general, tend to
improve the morals, and at the same time, to increase the happiness
of the soldiery, and must afford the most pure and rational enter-
tainment for every serious and well disposed mind," he wrote in his
General Orders of March 22, 1783. Those who have argued that
Washington was a fervent Christian have usually quoted, too, his
First Inaugural (1789) and his Farewell Address (1796), in both of
which he made a strong case for religious faith and practice as the
basis of public and private good. But again, it should be stressed that
the *nature* of the religion Washington advocated in these addresses is
specifically left vague—and also, not least, that the Farewell Address
was actually written by Alexander Hamilton, a master in the use of
popular piety to serve political power, and largely based on the draft
of an earlier speech written by James Madison.

This, then, was George Washington: tolerant, latitudinarian, ut-
terly uninterested in theological niceties but firmly convinced that, in
the words of the First Inaugural, "there exists in the oeconomy and
course of nature, an indissoluble union between virtue [virtue, that
is, of the civic rather than theological variety] and happiness. . . ."
This is not exactly the George Washington we all learned about as

schoolchildren, a fact which is due, perhaps, to the timing of his death: 1799 marked the very end of the Enlightenment, the beginning of another wave of evangelism known as the Second Great Awakening, and the lead-up to the 1800 election, in which the godless candidate of the left, Jefferson, would be attacked by an increasingly evangelical opposition manipulated by the indefatigable Hamilton. After his death Washington was elevated by the partisan Federalist clergy to a high place alongside Moses and Noah as the inspired prophet and liberator of a chosen people.

One enterprising biographer, Mason Locke Weems, known to posterity as Parson Weems, was almost single-handedly responsible for creating the pious Washington of legend. Weems, an itinerant bookseller as well as a preacher, had a genius for pandering to the lowest common denominator and saw that there could be huge financial rewards in store for someone who could reinvent and market the Father of his Country in terms attractive to a mass readership.

> I've something to whisper in your lug [he wrote a friend in January, 1800]. Washington, you know is gone! Millions are gaping to read something about him. I am very nearly prim'd and cock'd for 'em. 6 months ago I set myself to collect anecdotes of him. My plan! I give his history, sufficiently minute—I accompany him from his start, thro the French & Indian & British or Revolutionary wars, to the Presidents chair, to the throne in the hearts of 5,000,000 of People. I then go on to show that his unparrelled [*sic*] rise & elevation were due to his Great Virtues.

As Marcus Cunliffe wrote in his introduction to a 1962 edition of Weems's *Life of Washington*,

> American nationalism was a self-conscious creation, and George Washington was its chief symbol. Traveling widely and continuously, Weems discovered by experiment what

Americans wanted to read. They were religiously minded, so they would buy Bibles, sermons, tracts. They were eager for color and excitement, so they would buy novels by the cartload. They were, when stimulated, ferociously patriotic, so they would buy works that ministered to their national pride. What better fare than the Weemsian biographies, which satisfied their wants—religion (or religiosity), romanticism, patriotism—simultaneously?

Has anything really changed from that day to this? Aren't these still the basic desires of the American public, and aren't Washington and the other Founding Fathers still being pressed into service as colorful exemplars of the Christian nation so many of our leaders endorse?

The first edition of Weems's biographical work appeared in 1800, only a few months after its subject's death. At first it was a mere pamphlet, but its success was so phenomenal that in the sixth edition (1808) it was expanded into a full-length book, *The Life of George Washington; With Curious Anecdotes, Equally Honourable to Himself and Exemplary to His Young Countrymen*. By 1825 it had gone into its twenty-ninth edition and had colored the entire culture and historical sensibility of early nineteenth-century America: the cherry-tree story, for instance, a complete fabrication, achieved universal fame and acceptance by its inclusion in the McGuffey *Reader*.

Weems enhanced his credibility by playing up a personal acquaintance with the great man that was probably an invention: he advertised himself as "formerly Rector of Mount-Vernon Parish," but only the Washingtons' neighbors would be aware that there was no such parish as "Mount-Vernon," and while it was true that Weems occasionally preached in Pohick Church, Truro Parish, there is no evidence that he ever did so with Washington in attendance.

Weems's *George Washington* scaled hyperbolic heights seldom if ever attempted in literature.

When the children of the years to come, hearing his great name re-echoed from every lip, shall say to their fathers, *"what was it that raised Washington to such heights of glory?"* let them be told that it was HIS GREAT TALENTS, CONSTANTLY GUIDED AND GUARDED BY RELIGION. For how shall man, *frail man,* prone to inglorious ease and pleasure, ever ascend the arduous steps of virtue, unless animated by the *mighty hopes* of religion? Or what shall stop him in his swift descent to infamy and vice, if unawed by that dread power which proclaims to the guilty that their secret crimes are seen, and shall not go unpunished?

This holy-rolling flavor permeates the entire biography and is comically at odds with the character of the real Washington, so self-contained and laconic.

Weems thought nothing of inventing incidents to bolster his case, and these episodes, unfortunately, became so famous through the wide dissemination of his book that they ended up as accepted components of the Washington myth. The cherry tree is one such tale; another is the iconic, but purely imaginary, image of Washington praying in the snow at Valley Forge, described by Weems as follows:

In the winter of '77, while Washington, with the American army lay encamped at Valley Forge, a certain good old FRIEND, of the respectable family name of Potts, if I mistake not, had occasion to pass through the woods near head-quarters. Treading his way along the venerable grove, suddenly he heard the sound of a human voice, which as he advanced increased on his ear, and at length became like the voice of one speaking much in earnest. As he approached the spot with a cautious step, whom should he behold, in a dark natural bower of ancient oaks, but the commander in chief of the American armies on his knees at prayer! Motionless with surprise, friend Potts continued on the place till the general, having ended his devotions, arose, and, with a countenance of angel serenity, retired to headquarters: friend Potts then went home, and on entering his parlour called out to his wife, "Sarah, my dear! Sarah! All's well! all's well! George Washington will yet prevail!

. . . He then related what he had seen, and concluded with this prophetical remark—"If George Washington be not a man of God, I am greatly deceived—and still more shall I be deceived if God do not, through him, work out a great salvation for America."

This inspirational scene became a standard subject for various hack painters of the time; so, too, did Weems's fabulously ridiculous description of Washington's death (the following brief digest is pared down from a four-page account):

Feeling that the hour of his departure out of this world was at hand, he desired that every body would quit the room. They all went out, and according to his wish, left him—with his God.

There, by himself, like Moses alone on the top of Pisgah, he seeks the face of God. There, *by himself,* standing as on the awful boundary that divides time from eternity, that separates this world from the next, he cannot quit the long-frequented haunts of the one, nor launch away into the untried regions of the other, until (in humble imitation of the world's great Redeemer) he has poured forth into the bosom of his God those strong sensations which the solemnity of his situation naturally suggested.

. . . Feeling that the silver chord of life is loosing, and that his spirit is ready to quit her old companion the body, he extends himself on his bed—closes his eyes for the *last* time, with his own hands—folds his arms decently on his breast, then breathing out *"Father of mercies! take me to thyself,"*—he fell asleep.

Swift on angels' wings the brightening saint ascended;
while voices more than human were heard (*in Fancy's ear*)
warbling through the happy regions, and hymning the great
procession towards the gates of heaven. His glorious coming
was seen far off, and myriads of mighty angels hastened forth,
with golden harps, to welcome the honored stranger. High in
front of the shouting hosts, were seen the beauteous forms of
FRANKLIN, WARREN, MERCER, SCAMMEL, and of him who fell
at Quebec, with all the virtuous patriots, who, on the side of
Columbia, toiled or bled for *liberty* and *truth*. . . .

One is especially amused to spot Franklin among the heavenly
throng.

Countless kitschy paintings of this event were perpetrated.
Washington's ascent to heaven soon became a popular motif in
American folk art, an integral part of the "idolatrous worship" of
Washington which that irreverent pair of cronies, Benjamin Rush
and John Adams, mocked in their correspondence of 1812, with
Rush confessing himself disgusted by "the impious application of
names and epithets to him which are ascribed in Scripture only to
God and to Jesus Christ."

Weems's version of Washington and subsequent hagiographies
buried the real man so deeply that we have yet to succeed in digging
him out. As one Washington biographer, William Roscoe Thayer,
wrote in 1922, "Owing to the pernicious drivel of . . . Weems no
other great man in history has had to live down such a mass of absurdities and deliberate false inventions. At last after a century and a
quarter the rubbish has been mostly cleared away. . . ."

Thayer was too optimistic: more than eighty years after he wrote,
much rubbish is still left to be cleared away, and modern versions of
Parson Weems are doing all they can to heap on more. Jerry Falwell,
Pat Robertson, and other influential ministers use the internet as well
as the pulpit to assure Americans that the father of their country was

a passionately devout Christian, while powerful politicians such as George W. Bush, John Ashcroft, and Newt Gingrich echo their fundamentalist rhetoric. Washington's habitual reserve has not made the serious historian's task any easier: unlike Adams, Rush, Franklin, Jefferson, Gouverneur Morris, and other key Founding Fathers, who carried on lively and exceedingly frank correspondences with close friends, Washington maintained his air of formality with all but a very few. His general silence on the subject of Christianity, however, is highly suggestive. If he had been a Christian believer he would have had nothing to lose by saying so, while if he had not been, he would have had a great deal to lose—he would, in Franklin's memorable phrase, merely be spitting against the wind.

CHAPTER THREE

Adams

"I mix religion with politics as little as possible."

—John Adams

※ IN 1820, as a very old man, John Adams was asked by a clergyman to describe his attitude toward Calvinism. His response was
diplomatic but straightforward.

> I must be a very unnatural son to entertain any prejudices
> against the Calvinists, or Calvinism, according to your
> confession of faith; for my father and mother, my uncles and
> aunts, and all my predecessors, from our common ancestor,
> who landed in this country two hundred years ago, wanting
> five months, were of that persuasion. Indeed, I have never
> known any better people than the Calvinists. Nevertheless, I
> must acknowledge that I cannot class myself under that
> denomination.

Like Benjamin Franklin, Adams was raised a Calvinist, in his case a
Congregationalist. But unlike Franklin, who remained astoundingly

and almost miraculously untouched by his religious education, Adams was deeply affected. During the course of his long life he would reject almost all of the theological tenets of his forefathers, but his personality and his habits were permanently marked by his Puritan heritage.

Duty, industry, responsibility: Adams took all these ideals extremely seriously and was perhaps the hardest-working and the most learned among the Founding Fathers, which is saying a great deal. Marital fidelity was also an important principle for him, and his long and happy marriage—more than a marriage, a true partnership—to Abigail Smith was the reward he reaped from its practice. (His prudish comments on what he perceived as the libertine morals of the French court in the 1770s make for amusing reading.) He strongly believed in the principle that felicity can be won only through virtue. "All sober inquirers after truth, ancient and modern, pagan and Christian," he wrote in his treatise "Thoughts on Government," "have declared that the happiness of man, as well as his dignity, consists in virtue." Unlike so many of us, who parrot this notion without taking the trouble to conform with it, Adams accepted it at face value and in consequence lived a visibly virtuous life—yes, and a happy one too.

But the enduring legacy of Adams's Puritan heritage, at least insofar as it affected American history and the philosophical dialogue that underlay the creation of the nation's governmental system, with its complex system of checks and balances, was his Calvinist sense of man's moral limitations. As he aged he stopped believing literally in the Fall of Adam and Eve as described in the Old Testament, but he retained a sense of man's essentially fallen nature and agreed with the arch-skeptic David Hume that reason is the slave of the passions—unlike the perpetually optimistic Jefferson, who in spite of all the evidence the age provided him with, never really gave up the Enlightenment hope that man was infinitely perfectible through the power of reason. ". . . [T]he nature of mankind is one thing, and the reason of mankind another," Adams wrote in *A Defence of the Constitutions of the United States of America* (1787–1788); "and the first has some relation to the last as the whole to a part: the passions and appetites are parts of human nature as well as reason and the moral sense. In the institution of government, it must be remembered, that although reason ought to govern individuals, it certainly never did since the Fall, and never will till the Millennium; and human nature must be taken as it is, as it has been, and will be." He said much the same thing, but more extensively, in a letter to Jefferson during the struggle for ratification of the United States Constitution:

> The Loss of Paradise, by eating a forbidden apple, has been many Thousand years a Lesson to Mankind; but not much regarded. Moral Reflections, wise Maxims, religious Terrors, have little Effect upon Nations when they contradict a present Passion, Prejudice, Imagination, Enthusiasm or Caprice. . . . I have long been settled in my own opinion, that neither Philosophy, nor Religion, nor Morality, nor Wisdom, nor Interest, will ever govern nations or Parties, against their Vanity, their Pride, their Resentment or Revenge, or their Avarice or Ambition. Nothing but Force and Power and Strength can restrain them.

Adams was a fourth-generation American whose distant forebear, Henry Adams, had emigrated from England to Braintree, Massachusetts, in the seventeenth century. Born in 1735, the son of a cobbler and small farmer, John Adams entered Harvard at the age of fifteen with the intention of studying for the ministry. He might have continued on this track but he was not inspired by what he observed of church politics in his hometown. The minister at the Adams's own Braintree Congregationalist parish, one Lemuel Briant, shocked the town fathers with his liberal leanings toward Arminianism and Unitarianism, and in 1749 he preached a sermon on "The Absurdity and Blasphemy of Deprecating Moral Virtue" that denied the Calvinist tenets of original sin and election. This created a furor, with many prominent citizens calling for Briant's dismissal, though in the end the parish decided to retain him. The whole fracas gave Adams an unedifying glimpse of what he would later call "a Spirit of Dogmatism and Bigotry in Clergy and Laity," and he had no wish to confront it in his own professional life. This brush with the seamier side of public religion was similar to that which Franklin had encountered in the Hemphill affair, and had similar effects on Adams, turning him, like Franklin, definitively away from theological controversy as essentially unimportant and needlessly destructive of the community and body politic.

The intellectual currents of the time, too, helped direct Adams's interests away from the ministry. Soon he was soaking up "natural philosophy" (science) and political philosophy, notably the revolutionary works of Locke, Bolingbroke, and Montesquieu, and beginning to question the strict tenets of his fathers' faith. The result was that he changed his focus of study from theology to the law. He was presented for admission at the Boston bar at the age of twenty-three. By the 1760s he had developed a "natural law" philosophy derived from political theorists like Locke, Pufendorf, and Algernon Sidney: human rights, in this view, are inherent and derive from the "Creator" (as opposed to the more loaded term "God")—a concept Jefferson would enshrine in the Declaration of Independence ("They are endowed by their Creator with certain unalienable rights"). Hence from Adams's *Dissertation of Canon and Feudal Law* (1765): "*Rights*, that cannot be repealed or restrained by human laws— *Rights*, derived from the great Legislator of the universe. . . . [G]overnment [is] a plain, simple, intelligible thing, founded in nature and reason, and quite comprehendible by common sense."

Adams's letters and diary entries of the 1770s, during which time he became identified with the fight for American independence, show a struggle in which the provincial religious prejudices of his youth slowly give way to the tolerance typical of the international Enlightenment. As a delegate to the First Continental Congress in 1774, this small-town New Englander explored Philadelphia's wide opportunities for religious experience with a distinct sense of adventure:

> This day I went to Dr. Allison's meeting in the forenoon, and heard the Dr.; a good discourse upon the Lord's supper. This is a Presbyterian meeting. I confess I am not fond of the Presbyterian meetings in this town. I had rather go to Church [that is, Church of England, or Episcopalian services]. We have better sermons, better prayers, better speakers, softer, sweeter music, and genteeler company. And I must confess that the Episcopal Church is quite as agreeable to my taste as the Presbyterian. They are both slaves to the domination of the priesthood. I like the Congregational way best, next to that the Independent.

But his tolerance, at that early period, extended only so far. He went on to describe a Catholic service, and his comments on this subject are worth quoting because they epitomize the prevalent Calvinist prejudices against the Roman church and show how essentially conventional Adams still was at that time.

> This afternoon, led by curiosity and good company, I strolled away to mother church, or rather to grandmother church. I mean the Romish chapel. I heard a good, short moral essay upon the duty of parents to their children, founded in justice and charity, to take care of their interests, temporal and spiritual. This afternoon's entertainment was to me most awful and affecting; the poor wretches fingering their beads, chanting Latin not a word of which they understood; their pater nosters and ave Marias; their holy water; their crossing themselves perpetually; their bowing to the name of Jesus, whenever they hear it; their bowings and kneelings and

genuflections before the altar. The dress of the priest was rich with lace. His pulpit was velvet and gold. The altarpiece was very rich; little images and crucifixes about; wax candles lighted up. But how shall I describe the picture of our saviour in a frame of marble over the altar, at full length, upon the cross in the agonies, and the blood dropping and streaming from his wounds! The music, consisting of an organ and a choir of singers, went all the afternoon except sermon time. And the assembly chanted most sweetly and exquisitely.

Here is everything which can lay hold of the eye, ear, and imagination—everything which can charm and bewitch the simple and ignorant. I wonder how Luther ever broke the spell.

Unlike the Constitutional Convention thirteen years later, the First Continental Congress made a formal appeal for divine aid. This fact is often cited by modern proponents of public prayer as evidence that the Founding Fathers intended the American government to be a Christian one, but what is really significant is not so much that the Congress of 1774 opened with a prayer—for considering the times, that was only to be expected—but that the Constitutional Convention of 1787, by general consent, did not. The climate of opinion had greatly changed during those thirteen years.

In any case that the First Continental Congress would make an appeal to the Deity was by no means a foregone conclusion, as a letter Adams wrote to his wife shows.

When the Congress first met, Mr. Cushing made a motion that it should be opened with prayer. It was opposed by Mr. Jay, of New York, and Mr. Rutledge, of South Carolina, because we were so divided in religious sentiments, some Episcopalians, some Quakers, some Anabaptists, some Presbyterians, and some Congregationalists, that we could not join in the same act of worship. Mr. Samuel Adams arose and said he was no bigot, and could hear a prayer from a gentleman of piety and virtue, who was at the same time a friend to his country. He was a stranger in Philadelphia, but had heard that Mr. Duché (Dushay they pronounce it) deserved that character, and therefore he moved that Mr. Duché, an Episcopal clergyman, might be desired to read prayers to the Congress, to-morrow morning. The motion was seconded and passed in the affirmative. Mr. Randolph, our president, waited on Mr. Duché, and received for answer that if his health would permit he certainly would. Accordingly, next morning he appeared with his clerk and in his pontificals, and read several prayers in the established form; and then read the Collect for the seventh day of September, which was the thirty-fifth Psalm. You must remember this was the next morning after we heard the horrible rumor of the cannonade of Boston. I never saw a greater effect upon an audience. It seemed as if Heaven had ordained that Psalm to be read on that morning.

After this, Mr. Duché, unexpected to everybody, struck out into an extemporary prayer, which filled the bosom of every man present. I must confess I never heard a better prayer, or one so well pronounced. Episcopalian as he is, Dr. Cooper [the Rev. Samuel Cooper, minister of the Brattle Street Church in Boston] himself never prayed with such fervor, such ardor, such earnestness and pathos, and in language so elegant and sublime—for America, for the Congress, for the Province of Massachusetts Bay, and especially the town of Boston. It has had an excellent effect upon everybody here.

The ecumenical spirit of the Congress infected Adams. In 1775 he still expressed his preference for the New England colonies, whose institutions "for the Support of Religion, Morals, and De-cency exceed any other; obliging every Parish to have a Minister, and every Person to go to Meeting, &c," but decades later we find him inveighing against the same system as bigoted and tyrannical, and remarking acidly that "a change in the solar system might be expected as soon as a change in the ecclesiastical system of Massachusetts." An opening prayer by an inspirational preacher, as in 1774, was one thing: the intrusion of religion into government and the battles between sects and factions that inevitably follow in the wake of such intrusions was something else. One of the delegates at the Second Continental Congress in 1775 was a clergyman, a Doctor Zubly of Georgia, who wanted the group to focus specifically upon America's Christian identity. Adams respected Zubly as "a man of learning and ingenuity" but confided to Abigail that

> as he is the first gentleman of the cloth who has appeared in Congress, I cannot but wish he may be the last. Mixing the sacred character with that of the statesman, as it is quite unnecessary at this time of day, in these colonies, is not attended with any good effects. The clergy are universally too little acquainted with the world and the modes of business, to engage in civil affairs with any advantage. Besides, those of them who are really men of learning, have conversed with books so much more than men as to be too much loaded with vanity to be good politicians.

A passionate student of history, Adams was always conscious that whenever and wherever temporal and spiritual power had joined forces the people's rights were trampled upon. Discussing the nature of tyranny with Benjamin Rush, he opined that "Aristocratical tyrants are the worst species of all; and sacerdotal tyrants have been the worst of aristocratical tyrants in all ages and nations." He believed, at least during the years he spent helping to form the new nation, that it was man's duty to worship "the Creator," but strongly affirmed the right of each individual to define that Creator, and to worship him, in his or her own way—a position directly derived from John Locke's *Letter Concerning Toleration*. As a result Adams was a firm friend to religious liberty and a supporter of disestablishment throughout his career.

What is truly interesting about Adams's religious views is that as he aged and developed they became less and less doctrinaire, even less and less specifically Christian. Some have considered Adams to have been the wisest of the Founding Fathers, and if wisdom consists in an open mind, a revulsion against strict doctrine, and a corresponding suspicion of idealistic and utopian schemes, this is a reasonable contention. In 1810 he wrote, "Ask me not, then, whether I am a Catholic or Protestant, Calvinist or Arminian. As far as they are Christians, I wish to be a fellow-disciple with them all. . . ." He knew what he was talking about, having spent a lifetime in study. "For more than sixty Years I have been attentive to this great Subject [religion]," he wrote in old age. "Controversies, between Calvinists and Arminians, Trinitarians and Unitarians, Deists and Christians, Atheists and both, have attracted my Attention, whenever the singular Life I have lead would admit, to all these questions. . . . I think, I can now say I have read away Bigotry, if not Enthusiasm."

What were the results of Adams's researches? His correspondence with Thomas Jefferson between 1812 and 1826, now available in a one-volume edition, is wonderfully honest and revealing: retired from the political fray and writing in confidence to each other purely as private citizens, the two old men at last felt able to state their beliefs frankly. Here, in 1816, Adams writes:

> For the last Year or two I have devoted my self to this kind of [theological] Study: and have read 15 Volumes of Grim,* Seven Volumes of Tuckers Neddy Search and 12 Volumes of Dupuis† besides a 13th of plates and Tracey's Analysis,‡ and 4 Volumes of Jesuitical History! Romances all! I have learned

---

*Baron Friedrich Melchior von Grimm, *Correspondence* (1812–1813).
†Charles Francois Dupuis, *Origine de tous les cultes.* . . . (1795).
‡Comte Destutt de Tracy, *Commentaries on Montesquieu* (1811).

nothing of importance to me, for they have made no Change in
my moral or religious Creed, which has for 50 or 60 Years
been contained in four short Words *"Be just and good."* In this
result they all agree with me. . . . My Conclusion from all of
them is Universal Tolleration.

Lest we should assume Adams expected such toleration to be
confined to Christians alone, let us look at a letter he wrote only two
weeks later, which contains one of the most eloquent and humane
statements he ever made:

> Phylosophy is not only the love of Wisdom, but the Science
> of the Universe and its Cause. There is, there was and there
> will be but one Master of Phylosophy in the Universe.
> Portions of it, in different degrees are revealed to Creatures.
> Phylosophy looks with an impartial Eye on all terrestrial
> religions.

Adams's own preferred form of worship may have been Christianity—
he remained what he called "a church-going animal" all his life—but
he did not proselytize, or seek to impose Christianity on the rest of the
world. He satisfied his own "church-going" instincts with a formal adherence to Unitarianism, the least dogmatic and least specifically
"Christian" sect within the Christian religion.

"Phylosophy looks with an impartial eye on all terrestrial religions": Adams implicitly admitted that had he been born in a different time and place he would probably have practiced some other
faith, and he quoted with approval Hesiod's pragmatic injunction to
"Honour the Gods established by law." "I know not how We can escape Martyrdom, without a discreet Attention to this praecept," he
told Jefferson. "You have suffered, and I have suffered more than
You, for want of a strict if not a due Observance of this Rule."

He heartily concurred with Jefferson's distaste for prophets and
revelation, which would seem to have made much of the Bible prob-

lematic for him. All the revelation we need is contained, he believed, in nature and in our own power of reason, and can be comprehended without any recourse to mysticism. The Athanasian Creed and the concept of the Trinity he found simply absurd.

> The human Understanding is a revelation from its Maker which can never be disputed or doubted. There can be no Scepticism, Pyrrhonism, or Incredulity or Infidelity here. No Prophecies, no Miracles are necessary to prove this celestial communication. This revelation has made it certain that two and one make three; and that one is not three; nor can three be one. We can never be so certain of any Prophecy; or of any miracle, or the design of any miracle as We are, from the revelation of nature i.e. natures God that two and two are equal to four. Miracles or Prophecies might frighten Us out of our Witts; might scare us to death; might induce Us to lie; to say that We believe that 2 and 2 make 5. But We should not believe it. We should know the contrary.

> Had you and I been forty days with Moses on Mount Sinai and admitted to behold, the divine Shekinah, and there told that one was three and three, one: We might not have had courage to deny it, but We could not have believed it. The thunders and Lightenings and Earthqu[ak]es and the transcendant Splendors and Glories, might have overwhelmed Us with terror and Amazement: but We could not have believed the doctrine.

Hence his adherence to Unitarianism, which denied the doctrine of the Trinity and the divinity of Christ. Adams, along with Jefferson, Joseph Priestley, and other freethinkers of the time, believed that the doctrines of Christianity were simple in conception but had been hopelessly corrupted by the various creeds and philosophies that had been grafted onto them. Platonic mysticism, which they felt had nothing to do with Christ's essentially moral teachings, was seen as especially pernicious. Adams disliked the Platonic elements of Christianity and recalled his own perusal of Plato with extreme distaste: ". . . I labored through the tedious toil. My disappointment was very great, my Astonishment was greater and my disgust was shocking. Two things only did I learn from him. 1. that Franklins Ideas of exempting Husbandmen and Mariners etc. from the depradations of War were borrowed from him. 2. That Sneezing is a cure for the Hickups."

As for prophets, Adams thought them a pesky and dangerous breed, capable of stirring up infinite trouble and appealing to the worst and lowest parts of the human animal. Recalling the fact that the prophet Jeremiah had been punished by being put in stocks, Adams commented that

> It may be thought impiety by many, but I could not help wishing that the ancient practice had been continued down to more modern times and that all the Prophets at least from Peter the Hermit*, to Nimrod Hews† inclusively had been confined in the Stocks and been prevented from spreading so many delusions and shedding so much blood. Could you believe that the mad rant of Nimrod which was sent to me . . . and which I lent to a neighbor in whose house it was seen and read by some visitors, spread a great deal of terror and a serious apprehension that one third of the human race would be destroyed on the fourth day of the next month?

Adams would obviously have been appalled by the widespread millennialism of our own era, and astounded at the percentage of the American population who now eagerly await the Rapture.

---

*Preacher of the "People's Crusade," an army of peasants who made up part of the First Crusade at the end of the eleventh century.

†Nimrod Hughes was a Virginia prophet who had predicted that one-third of mankind would perish on June 4, 1812.

So Adams's religion—seeing revelation in nature and in man's capacity to reason, worshiping a benign, nondenominational deity rather than the jealous Old Testament God—was not so very different in the end from the outspoken deism of Paine or Jefferson. But Adams always took a much darker view of the human race than they did. Lapsed Calvinist though he was, he was still Calvinist enough to scoff at revolutionary France's utopian attempt to rid the country of the Catholic church and establish, in its place, a Temple of Reason. He admired reason as an abstract ideal but was not at all sure that it existed in a pure, disinterested form, still less that it could ever serve to control man's unruly passions.

> Perhaps We may laugh like the Angels in the French Fable. At a convivial repast of a Clubb of Choice Spirits of whom Gabriel and Michael were the most illustrious, after Nectar and Ambrosia had sett their hearts at ease, they began to converse upon the Mecanique Coeleste. After discussing the Zodiack and the Constellations and the Solar System they condescended to this Speck of dirt the Earth, and remarked some of its Inhabitants, the Lyon the Elephant the Eagle and even the Fidelity Gratitude and Adroitness of the Dog. At last one of them recollected Man. What a fine Countenance! What an elegant figure! What Subtility, Ingenuity, Versatillity Agility! And above all, *a rational Creature!* At this the whole board broke out into a broad Ha! Ha! Ha! That resounded through the Vault of Heaven: exclaiming *"Man a rational Creature!"* How could any rational Being even dream that Man was a rational Creature?

This philosophically disabused man, unable to deceive himself on the subject of human nature, simply could not bring himself to look at the future with anything but trepidation. He wished his Virginian friends the best of luck as they planned their unprecedentedly secular educational institution, the University of Virginia, but took leave to doubt whether it could remain untouched by the passions of sect and faction. "I wish you, Mr. Madison and Mr. Monroe Success in Your Collegiate institution," he wrote Jefferson. "And I wish that Superstition in Religion exciting Superstition in Politicks, and both united in directing military Force, alias glory may never blow up all your benevolent and phylanthropic Lucubrations. But the History of all Ages is against you." On a lunacy scale he ranked the optimistic (and often atheistic) *philosophes* as about equal with apocalyptically minded Christians. "I leave those profound Phylosophers whose sagacity perceives the Perfectability of Humane Nature, and those illuminated Theologians who expect the Apocalyptic Reign, to enjoy their transporting hopes; provided always that they will not engage Us in Crusades and French Revolutions, nor burn Us for doubting."

But though reason was tenuous at best, its alternatives, fanaticism and bigotry, were unthinkable. The older Adams got, the more disgusted he became with religious fundamentalism, particularly the New England variety in which he had been brought up. Speaking confidentially of the Essex Junto (a coalition of politically conservative merchants and lawyers) and the fanatical breed of New England theologians, he dismissed them as "*Bos, fur, sus, atque sacerdos*, with a few bright exceptions" ["Ox, thief, pig, and priest"]. Addressing Jefferson, who had in 1817 complacently boasted that their country had averted a Protestant popedom, he exclaimed "Oh! Lord! Do you think that a Protestant Popedom is annihilated in America? Do you recollect, or have you ever attended to the ecclesiastical Strifes in Maryland Pensilvania, New York, and every part of New England? What a mercy it is that these People cannot whip and crop, and pillory and roast, *as yet* in the U.S.! If they could they would."

Adams had observed again and again that religious discord was possibly more destructive than any other variety to the public peace, and that an unscrupulous demagogue could manipulate religious passions to nefarious ends. "[T]here is a germ of religion in human nature so strong that whenever an order of men can persuade the people by flattery or terror that they have salvation at their disposal, there can be no end to fraud, violence, or usurpation," he commented.

This was an obvious danger during the highly religious period of the early nineteenth century; it continues to be just as much of a danger in our own, equally fervent, time. Adams's warnings are extraordinarily prescient and wise. Political thinkers like Madison and Jefferson strongly believed that the wide variety and number of religious sects in America, if equally tolerated, would create a balance of power so that no single one could ever dominate the others. Adams was not so sure. "The multitude and diversity of them, You will say, is our Security against them all. God grant it. But if We consider that the Presbyterians and Methodists are far the most numerous and the most likely to unite; let a George Whitefield arise, with a military cast, like Mahomet, or Loyola, and what will become of all the other Sects who can never unite?" In other words, if a religious genius on the level of Whitefield who was also a military or political genius were to come along, the tenuous balance of religious power would end abruptly.

That has not happened so far, but the grimly realistic Adams would have been unsurprised by what *has* happened in this country: the creation of a vast evangelical voting bloc, with all the fundamentalist sects effectively courted and won by a single political party. Adams rarely allowed himself the luxury of optimism and was painfully aware of every pitfall that faced the infant republic.

Religious Controversies, and Ecclesiastical Contests are as common and will be as Sharp as any in civil Politicks foreign, or domestick. In what sense and to what extent the Bible is Law, may give rise to as many doubts and quarrells as any of our civil political military or maritime Laws and will intermix with them to irritate Factions of every sort. I dare not look beyond my Nose into futurity. Our Money, our Commerce, our Religion, our National and state Constitutions, even our

Arts and Sciences, are so many seed Plotts of Division, Faction, Sedition and Rebellion. Every thing is transmuted into an Instrument of Electioneering. Election is the grand Brama, the immortal Lama, I had almost said, the Jaggernaught, for Wives are almost ready to burn upon the Pile and Children to be thrown under the Wheel.

Both as president from 1796 to 1800 and as an unsuccessful presidential candidate in 1800, when as the incumbent he lost to Jefferson, Adams had personally suffered considerable political fallout due to the high emotions any whiff of religious controversy always tends to stir up. It is fascinating to read his comments on the subject since (like so much of what he wrote) they are so perfectly applicable to the rage and paranoia that arises when church/state issues are challenged today. In 1798 Adams had recommended a national fast (comparable in today's terms to a day of prayer) when the country seemed to be on the brink of war with revolutionary France. This action, he later claimed, "turned me out of office."

A general suspicion prevailed that the Presbyterian Church was ambitious and aimed at an establishment as a national church. I was represented as a Presbyterian and at the head of this political and ecclesiastical project. The secret whisper ran through all the sects, "Let us have Jefferson, Madison, Burr, anybody, whether they be philosophers, Deists, or even atheists, rather than a Presbyterian President." This principle is at the bottom of the unpopularity of national fasts and thanksgivings. Nothing is more dreaded than the national government meddling with religion. This wild letter, I very much fear, contains seeds of an ecclesiastical history of the U.S. for a century to come.

Well, more than a century, obviously. "Nothing is more dreaded than the national government meddling with religion": this is still true, and accounts for what strike so many as gross overreaction against school prayer, creches in public spaces, and other encroachments. The historical and psychological origins of this dread are well worth remembering.

All this helps explain why the non-Christian Jefferson, of all people, was the presidential winner at the very moment the Second Great Awakening was sweeping the country, and why this Enlightenment skeptic and radical was the preferred candidate of the Methodists and the Baptists, large denominations that had always felt excluded from social and political power. Better a president with no religion, these reasoned, than one of a different, and ascendant, one, for an irreligious president would be more likely to protect the rights of religious minorities than a member (even a former member, in Adams's case) of a dominant, and traditionally intolerant, American sect.

In spite of the Bill of Rights and the legal framework the founders had created to protect freedom of religion and of the press, Adams felt that social pressures, or what was already beginning to be referred to as the court of public opinion, unfortunately made these freedoms ideal abstractions rather than firm realities. Transforming such ideals into realities would be a task for future generations. "I cannot contemplate human Affairs without laughing or crying," he wrote Jefferson in 1817. "I choose to laugh. When People talk of the Freedom of Writing Speaking or thinking, I cannot choose but laugh. No such thing ever existed. No such thing now exists: but I hope it will exist. But it must be hundreds of years after you and I shall write and speak no more." Only a year before his death he was still expounding on the subject.

> We think ourselves possessed or at least we boast that we are so of Liberty of conscience on all subjects and of the right of free inquiry and private judgement, in all cases and yet how far are we from these exalted privileges in fact. There exists I

believe throughout the whole Christian world a law which makes it blasphemy to deny or doubt the divine inspiration of all the books of the old and new Testaments from Genesis to Revelations. In most countries of Europe it is punished by fire at the stake, or the rack or the wheel: in England itself it is punished by boring through the tongue with a red hot poker: in America it is not much better. . . . A law was made in the latter end of the last century repealing the cruel punishments of the former laws but substituting fine and imprisonment upon all those blasphemers upon any book of the old Testament or new. Now what free inquiry when a writer must surely encounter the risk of fine or imprisonment for adducing any argument for investigation into the divine authority of those books? . . . I think such laws a great embarassment, great obstructions to the improvement of the human mind. Books that cannot bear examination certainly ought not to be established as divine inspiration by penal laws. It is true few persons appear desirous to put such laws in execution and it is also true that some few persons are hardy enough to venture to depart from them; but as long as they continue in force as laws the human mind must make an awkward and clumsy progress in its investigations. I wish they were repealed.

Adams viewed with some dismay the rise of religious fundamentalism that took place during the early nineteenth century: "Instead of the most enlightened people, I fear we Americans shall soon have the character of the silliest people under Heaven," he fretted. Meanwhile, observing the activities of the Congress of Vienna in 1815 as it restored ancient monarchies in Napoleon's former domains and, with them, the all-powerful Catholic church, he worried that the clock was being turned hopelessly back. A political radical but not a social or religious one, Adams had disapproved of much of the

French *philosophes'* program; still, he knew that he himself was very much a product of the international Enlightenment.

[A]ccording to the few lights that remain to Us, We may say that the Eighteenth Century, notwithstanding all its Errors and Vices, has been, of all that are past, the most honourable to human Nature. Knowledge and Virtues were increased and diffused, Arts, Sciences useful to Men, ameliorating their condition, were improved, more than in any former equal Period.

But, what are We to say now? Is the Nineteenth Century to be a Contrast to the Eighteenth? Is it to extinguish all the Lights of its Predecessors? Are the Sorbonne, the Inquisition, the Index expurgatorious, and the Knights Errant of St Ignatius Loyola to be revived and restored to all their salutary Powers of supporting and propagating the mild Spirit of Christianity?

Essentially a man of both faith and reason, Adams reconciled the two sides of his character in his allegiance to the Unitarian Church, which required little of its adherents in the way of dogma save a belief in a supreme deity. This sect suited Adams's beliefs, which became ever more nebulous as time went on. The more he studied, the less he felt sure of; the longer he lived, the shorter grew his creed. In 1812 he wrote:

I am weary of contemplating nations from the lowest and most beastly degradations of human Life, to the highest Refinements of Civilization: I am weary of Philosophers, Theologians, Politicians, and Historians. They are immense Masses of Absurdities, Vices and Lies. Montesquieu had sense enough to say in Jest, that all our Knowledge might be comprehended in twelve Pages in Duodecimo: and, I believe him, in earnest. I could express my Faith in shorter terms. He who loves the Workman and his Work, and who does what he can to preserve and improve it, shall be accepted of him.

Any further speculation was idle. Adams had spent a very long lifetime seeking knowledge and enlightenment, but he finally came to believe these goals were beyond human grasp and likely to remain so. "That there is an active principle of power in the Universe is apparent," he reflected a year before his death, "but in what substance that active principle power resides, is past our investigation. The faculties of our understanding are not adequate to penetrate the Universe. Let us do our duty which is, to do as we would be done by, and that one would think, could not be difficult, if we honestly aim at it." The Golden Rule, then, comprises the pure essence of moral philosophy.

Adams continued to believe in the immortality of the soul but cheerfully admitted that he could find no rationale for this faith. In any case, reflections on the subject did not bother him much, for as he pointed out, "if we are disappointed we shall never know it." In early 1826 he wrote:

> I am certainly very near the end of my life. I am far from
> trifling with the idea of Death which is a great and solemn
> event. But I contemplate it without terror or dismay, "aut
> transit, aut finit" [either it is a transformation, or it is the end],
> if finit, which I cannot believe, and do not believe, there is an
> end of all but I shall never know it, and why should I dread it,
> which I do not; if transit I shall ever be under the same
> condition and administration of Government in the Universe,
> and I am not afraid to trust and confide in it.

There was no assurance to be had, no infallible dogma: one had simply to submit to one's unknown fate with trust and humility. By the end of his life Adams had abandoned all certainty on religious matters. Sometimes he sounded almost as skeptical as David

Hume, and as wholly open-minded. "This world," he stated with a certain bemusement, "is a mixture of the Sublime and the beautiful, the base and contemptible, the whimsical and ridiculous, (According to our narrow Sense; and triffling Feelings). It is a Riddle and an Enigma."

CHAPTER FOUR

Jefferson

"History, I believe, furnishes no example of a priest-
ridden people maintaining a free civil government."

—Thomas Jefferson

🐦 AS THE AUTHOR of the Declaration of Independence, Thomas
Jefferson secured himself a preeminent position in the American pan-
theon despite personal principles that have been distasteful to Christians throughout our history. Defamed by the religious right of his
day as the Virginia Voltaire, Jefferson, like Franklin, was a true Enlightenment *philosophe* in every sense of the word, a thorough skeptic
who valued reason far above faith and subjected every religious tradition, including his own, to scientific scrutiny. Contemporary Christian conservatives such as Timothy Dwight, the president of Yale
University during Jefferson's presidency, castigated him as a Jacobin
in politics and an arch-infidel who would drag the country into a mire
of sin and corruption.

He had earned their enmity for three reasons: first, for writing
the Virginia Statute for Religious Freedom, a radical and ground-
breaking document that would eventually serve as the model for the

legal principle of church/state separation that still obtains in America today; second, as the first and most influential American advocate of the French science and philosophy that was so widely perceived at that time as atheistic; and third, as the author of *Notes on the State of Virginia*, a classic of eighteenth-century freethinking. This 1784 document created an outrage among the religiously minded that could sometimes reach hysterical levels. Consider one extract, which takes John Locke's principles much further than Locke himself ever ventured to take them and whose language seems almost deliberately calculated to provoke the zealots of the time:

> The error seems not sufficiently eradicated, that the operations of the mind, as well as the acts of the body, are subject to the coercion of the laws. . . . The legitimate powers of government extend to such acts only as are injurious to others. But it does me no injury for my neighbor to say there are twenty gods, or no God. It neither picks my pocket nor breaks my leg. . . . reason and free inquiry are the only effectual agents against error. . . . They are the natural enemies of error, and of error only.

If Jefferson intended to stir things up he certainly succeeded, and this passage soon became notorious. The response of the Reverend William Linn, a Dutch Reformed minister from New York, was typical: "Let my neighbor once persuade himself that there is no God, and he will soon pick my pocket, and break not only my *leg* but my *neck*. If there be no God, there is no law." Linn was expressing what was surely the majority opinion, and probably still is—that human nature *requires* religion as a guarantee for morally correct behavior. Jefferson clearly was not of this school of thought. A conclusion that many inevitably drew was that Jefferson was an atheist, though he did not define himself as one, at least not in writing. But it is safe to say that he was definitely not a Christian, for while Jefferson professed to revere Jesus Christ as a philosopher and moralist he displayed nothing but contempt for the Christian religion as it had been practiced and preached for nearly two millennia.

What are the self-selected Moral Majority, the legions of Americans who consider themselves "saved," to make of a revered Founding Father who referred to Christianity as "our particular superstition" and to the God of the Old Testament as "a being of terrific character, cruel, vindictive, capricious and unjust"? Jefferson openly professed an unadulterated disgust for clergymen of all denominations: "In every country and in every age," he wrote, "the priest has been hostile to liberty. He is always in alliance with the despot, abetting his abuses in return for protection to his own." It has been especially galling to believing Christians that this opinion was held by a man who was not only one of the key Founding Fathers but one of the great, acknowledged ornaments of American history and culture—"a fabulous polymath," in the words of the historian Bernard Bailyn: "politician, diplomat, architect, draftsman, connoisseur of painting, anthropologist, bibliophile, classicist, musician, lawyer, educator, oenologist, farm manager, agronomist, theologian (or rather, antitheologian), and amateur of almost every branch of science from astronomy to zoology, with special emphasis on paleontology."

Not being able to ignore Jefferson, the Christian right has decided to deliberately misinterpret his message. Anti-separationists deny that Jefferson's term "wall of separation between Church and State" meant anything like what modern "liberals" mean by the phrase. But if we read the whole passage from which this phrase was extracted, it really seems that he did:

> Believing with you that religion is a matter which lies solely
> between man and his God, that he owes account to none other
> for his faith or his worship, that the legislative powers of
> government reach actions only, and not opinions, I contemplate
> with sovereign reverence that act of the whole American people

which declared that their legislature should "make no law respecting an establishment of religion, or prohibiting the free exercise thereof," thus building *a wall of separation between Church and State* [italics mine]. (from his letter to the Committee of the Danbury Baptist Association, January 1, 1802)

Context is everything. Another famous phrase taken out of its proper context is the noble sentiment quoted on the wall of the Jefferson Memorial: "I have sworn upon the altar of God eternal hostility against every form of tyranny over the mind of man." Christian apologists disingenuously ask how a godless man could have said any such thing, and Newt Gingrich has even included this engraved quotation in his Christian tour of the District of Columbia. But again, the context tells us more than such zealots would like the gullible citizen to know: this quotation was actually taken from a characteristically Jeffersonian explosion against priests and clergymen. Mocking the clergy as "the *genus irritabile vatum*" (irritable tribe of priests), he complained during his 1800 presidential campaign that they had all entertained

a very favorite hope of obtaining an establishment of a particular form of Christianity through the United States; and as every sect believes its own form the true one, every one perhaps hoped for his own. . . . The returning good sense of our own country threatens abortion to their hopes, and they believe that any portion of power confided to me, will be exerted in opposition to their schemes. And they believe rightly: for *I have sworn upon the altar of God eternal hostility against every form of tyranny over the mind of man* [italics mine]. But this is all they have to fear from me: and enough too in their position.

In other words, the tyranny Jefferson struck out against was not that of political tyrants but of religious ones, not of kings but of ambitious clergymen jockeying for power and emoluments.

But what, Christians say, about the famous phrases of the Declaration of Independence: "the Laws of Nature and Nature's God," "They are endowed by their Creator with certain unalienable rights," and "firm reliance on the protection of divine Providence"? It should be remembered, first of all, that "Nature and Nature's God" was a standard formula employed not by conventional Christians but by Enlightenment deists: Nature's God was *not* the God of the Old Testament, whom Jefferson considered "cruel, vindictive, capricious and unjust." As for "a firm reliance on the protection of divine Providence," this phrase did not appear in Jefferson's draft; it was added later by Congress. Occasional references to Christianity as a "benign religion," as for example in the First Inaugural Address, appear to have been strictly *pro forma* examples of the pious hypocrisy politicians have practiced from time immemorial—for nothing the president ever wrote in private expressed a belief that institutionalized Christianity was benign. Quite the contrary, in fact.

Jefferson's natural inclination toward skepticism and empiricism was enhanced by upbringing, circumstances, and travel. Like George Washington, he was a product of the easygoing and undemanding Anglicanism practiced by the Virginia planter elite. He served on the church vestry when called upon to do so and in fact never officially abandoned the Episcopal church, though in later life he tended to identify himself as a Unitarian. But his church affiliation was strictly a formality—certainly a necessary one if he planned to continue in public life. As a youth he had read the writings of the deists along with refutations of them by various Anglican divines, and like Benjamin Franklin before him he quickly found himself far more in sympathy with the mild deist point of view than that of its doctrinaire opponents.

Jefferson's youthful perusal of the English deists and Commonwealth philosophers broadened his provincial American outlook; later, his five years' residence in France as American minister would broaden it still further. In Paris he frequented the salons of the *philosophes* and avidly participated in the intellectual debates of the time. He shared the belief of Diderot, Voltaire, and the other French *Encyclopédistes* that the world was a comprehensible place and that the application of reason—which Jefferson asserted was "the only oracle given you by heaven"—could not fail, in the long run, to explain its mysteries. He wholeheartedly agreed with his contemporary Diderot that "religion retreats as philosophy advances," and with the Marquis de Condorcet that Christianity "feared that spirit of investigation and doubt, that confidence in one's own reason, which is the scourge of all religious beliefs." His stated heroes were the stars of the Enlightenment firmament, and he commissioned the painter John Trumbull to paint for him likenesses of Bacon, Locke, and Newton, in his opinion "the three greatest men that have ever lived, without any exception, and as having laid the foundation of those super-structures which have been raised in the Physical and Moral Sciences." To name these three as the greatest men that had ever lived, without any exception, was an implicit criticism of great men of faith up to and including Jesus himself.

Jefferson followed the English liberal philosopher and deist, Henry St. John, Viscount Bolingbroke (who had a tremendous influence upon the founding generation), in maintaining that religion, like everything else in life, should be subjected to the test of reason—a tenet in direct opposition to the prevailing Calvinist emphasis on faith for its own sake. A famous letter to his nephew, Peter Carr, in which Jefferson offers the young man the benefit of his advice and experience, gives a pretty fair summary of his ideas on this subject.

> Religion. Your reason is now mature enough to examine this object. . . . [S]hake off all the fears, and servile prejudices, under which weak minds are servilely crouched. Fix reason firmly in her seat, and call to her tribunal every fact, every

opinion. Question with boldness even the existence of a God; because, if there be one, he must more approve of the homage of reason, than that of blindfolded fear. You will naturally examine first, the religion of your own country. Read the Bible, then, as you would read Livy or Tacitus. The facts which are within the ordinary course of nature, you will believe on the authority of the writer, as you do those of the same kind in Livy and Tacitus. The testimony of the writer weighs in their favor, in one scale, and their not being against the laws of nature, does not weigh against them. But those facts in the Bible which contradict the laws of nature, must be examined with more care, and under a variety of faces. Here you must recur to the pretensions of the writer to inspiration from God. Examine upon what evidence his pretensions are founded, and whether that evidence is so strong, as that its falsehood would be more improbable than a change in the laws of nature, in the case he relates. For example, in the book of Joshua, we are told, the sun stood still several hours. Were we to read that fact in Livy or Tacitus, we should class it with their showers of blood, speaking of statues, beasts, etc. But it is said, that the writer of that book was inspired. Examine, therefore, candidly, what evidence there is of his having been inspired. . . . You will next read the New Testament. It is the history of a personage called Jesus. Keep in your eye the opposite pretensions: 1, of those who say he was begotten by God, born of a virgin, suspended and reversed the laws of nature at will, and ascended bodily into heaven; and 2, of those who say he was a man of illegitimate birth, of a benevolent heart, enthusiastic mind, who set out without pretensions to divinity, ended in believing them, and was punished capitally for sedition, by being gibbeted, according to the Roman law, which punished the first commission of that offence by whipping, and the second by exile, or death *in furcâ*. . . .

Do not be frightened from this inquiry by any fear of its consequences. If it ends in a belief that there is no god, you will find incitements to virtue in the comforts and pleasantness you feel in its exercise, and the love of others which it will procure you. If you find reason to believe there is a God, a consciousness that you are acting under his eye, and that he approves you, will be a vast additional incitement; if that there be a future state, the hope of a happy existence in that increases the appetite to deserve it; if that Jesus was also a God, you will be comforted by a belief in his aid and love. In fine, I repeat, you must lay aside all prejudices on both sides, and neither believe nor reject anything, because any other persons, or description of persons, have rejected or believed it. Your own reason is the only oracle given you by heaven, and you are answerable, not for the rightness, but uprightness of the decision. I forgot to observe, when speaking of the New Testament, that you should read all the histories of Christ, as well as those whom a council of ecclesiastics have decided for us, to be pseudo-evangelists, as those they named Evangelists, Because these Pseudo-evangelists pretended to inspiration, as much as the others, and you are to judge their pretensions by your own reason, and not by the reason of those ecclesiastics.

This fascinating letter, a beautiful relic of Enlightenment empiricism, shows not only Jefferson's reverence for reason but his distrust—no, his downright distaste—for revelation, as he enjoins Carr to examine the Evangelists' claims to having been inspired. Jefferson's private opinions on the Revelation of St. John, expressed in a letter to Alexander Smyth, are characteristic, and worth quoting.

It is between 50. and 60. years since I read it, and I then considered it as merely the ravings of a Maniac, no more worthy, nor capable of explanation than the incoherences of our own nightly dreams. . . . I cannot so far respect them as to

consider them as an allegorical narrative of events, past or
subsequent. There is not enough coherence in them to
countenance any suite of rational ideas. . . . What has no
meaning admits no explanation. And pardon me if I say, with
the candor of friendship, that I think your time too valuable,
and your understanding of too high an order, to be wasted on
these paralogisms. You will perceive, I hope, also that I do not
consider them as revelations of the supreme being, whom I
would not so far blaspheme as to impute to him a pretension of
revelation, couched at the same time in terms which, he would
know, were never to be understood by those to whom they were
addressed.

The final sentence is in classic deist idiom, with its reference to a benign "supreme being" who could not possibly have any wish to needlessly mystify his creatures.

Jefferson's personal creed, as he described in confidence to trust-
worthy friends such as John Adams, Benjamin Waterhouse, Dr.
Joseph Priestley, and William Short, was a simple one. He believed,
in the deist manner, in one God, a benign creator whose only revelation to man is made through Nature and Reason. He believed, or
wished to believe (sometimes he didn't seem too sure), in an afterlife.
So far as Christian dogma goes, these two propositions are all that he
believed, and he listed under the category "artificial systems, invented by ultra-Christian sects," all the following doctrines: "The
immaculate conception of Jesus, His deification, the creation of the
world by Him, His miraculous powers, His resurrection and visible
ascension, His corporeal presence in the Eucharist, the Trinity, original sin, atonement, regeneration, election, orders or Hierarchy, etc."
"The day will come," he asserted (overoptimistically, as usual),
"when the mystical generation of Jesus, by the Supreme Being as his
father, in the womb of a virgin will be classed with the fable of the
generation of Minerva in the brain of Jupiter." He was particularly

scathing on the concept of the Trinity, scoffing at "the hocus-pocus phantasm of a God like another Cerberus, with one body and three heads, [which] had its birth and growth in the blood of thousands and thousands of martyrs. . . . In fact, the Athanasian paradox that one is three, and three but one, is so incomprehensible to the human mind, that no candid man can say he has any idea of it, and how can he believe what presents no idea?"

Jefferson could find no evidence whatever for Jesus' divinity, and ascribed Jesus' claim to being the son of God to an understandable state of mild delusion brought about by the overheated zealotry of his era.

> That Jesus did not mean to impose himself on mankind as the son of god physically speaking I have been convinced by the writings of men more learned than myself in that lore. But that he might conscientiously believe himself inspired from above, is very possible. The whole religion of the Jews, inculcated on him from his infancy, was founded in the belief of divine inspiration. . . . Elevated by the enthusiasm of a warm and pure heart, conscious of the high strains of an eloquence which had not been taught him, he might readily mistake the corruscations of his own fine genius for inspirations of an higher order. This belief carried therefore no more personal imputation, than the belief of Socrates, that himself was under the care and admonitions of a guardian daemon. And how many of our wisest men still believe in the reality of these inspirations while perfectly sane on all other subjects.

The use of the word "sane" in the final sentence says a great deal.

Jefferson considered, or claimed to consider, that the moral system taught by Jesus was "the most sublime and benevolent code of morals which has ever been offered to man," but believed that it had been distorted out of all recognition by a series of corrupters, most notably the four Evangelists, St. Paul, and John Calvin. This was a common opinion among deists, freethinkers, and theological liberals of the time. It was shared by Adams and, famously, by Priestley, whose books *The Corruptions of Christianity* and *Early Opinions of Jesus* had been enthusiastically read and hailed by Jefferson. The pure and simple philosophy of Jesus was comprehensible to any child, Jefferson said, but "the metaphysical abstractions of Athanasius, and the maniac ravings of Calvin, tinctured plentifully with the foggy dreams of Plato, have so loaded it with absurdities and incomprehensibilities, as to drive into infidelity men who had not the time, patience, or opportunity to strip it of it's meretricious trappings, and to see it in all it's native simplicity and purity."

In the draft of an 1809 letter to James Fishback, which he felt free to send only after excising this provocative material, Jefferson laid out his opinions in a rational and dispassionate tone.

Every religion consists of moral precepts, and of dogmas. In the first they all agree. All forbid us to murder, steal, plunder, bear false witness &ca. and these are the articles necessary for the preservation of order, justice, and happiness in society. In their particular dogmas all differ; no two professing the same. These respect vestments, ceremonies, physical opinions, and metaphysical speculations, totally unconnected with morality, and unimportant to the legitimate objects of society. Yet these are the questions on which have hung the bitter schisms of Nazarenes, Socinians, Arians, Athanasians in former times, and now of Trinitarians, Unitarians, Catholics, Lutherans, Calvinists, Methodists, Baptists, Quakers & c. Among the Mahometans we are told that thousands fell victims to the dispute whether the first or second toe of Mahomet was longest; and what blood, how many human lives have the words "this do in remembrance of me" cost the Christian world! We all agree in the obligation of the moral precepts of Jesus; but we schismatize and lose ourselves in subtleties about

his nature, his conception maculate or immaculate, whether he
was a god or not a god, whether his votaries are to be initiated
by simple aspersion, by immersion, or without water; whether
his priests must be robed in white, in black, or not robed at all;
whether we are to use our own reason, or the reason of others,
in the opinions we form, or as to the evidence we are to believe.
It is on questions of this, and still less importance, that such
oceans of human blood have been spilt, and whole regions of
the earth have been desolated by wars and persecutions, in
which human ingenuity has been exhausted in inventing new
tortures for their brethren. It is time then to become sensible
how insoluble these questions are by minds like ours, how
unimportant, and how mischievous; and to consign them to the
sleep of death, never to be awakened from it. . . . We see good
men in all religions, and as many in one as in another. It is then a
matter of principle with me to avoid disturbing the tranquility
of others by the expression of any opinion on the [unimportant
points] innocent questions on which we schismatize, and think
it enough to hold fast to those moral precepts which are of the
essence of Christianity, and of all other religions.

"Unimportant points" in the last sentence was softened into "innocent questions," but it is clear by Jefferson's dismissive tone here and
elsewhere that he did find such points entirely unimportant, if not
downright ridiculous.

Jefferson was blistering in his attack on many of the eminent figures of the Christian faith in their role as "corrupters." "Of this band
of dupes and imposters, Paul was the great Corypheus, and first cor-
rupter of the doctrines of Jesus," he asserted. Not far behind Paul
were the Evangelists, ignorant and superstitious men who distorted
their supposed Messiah's message. "If we could believe that he [Je-
sus] really countenanced the follies, the falsehoods, and the charla-
tanism which his biographers [Matthew, Mark, Luke, and John]

father on him, and admit the misconstructions, interpolations, and theorizations of the fathers of the early, and the fanatics of the latter ages, the conclusion would be irresistible by every sound mind that he was an imposter."

In a series of private reflections to Adams, Jefferson upheld the opinion of the philosopher William Enfield that the Jewish moral philosophy of Jesus' era had reached a "low state" of "wretched depravity," and that Jesus saw himself as essentially an agent of moral reform. But "In extracting the pure principles which he taught," Jefferson reiterates,

> we should have to strip off the artificial vestments in which they have been muffled by priests, who have travestied them into various forms, as instruments of riches and power to them. We must dismiss the Platonists and Plotinists, the Stagyrites and Gamalielites, the Eclectics the Gnostics and Scholastics, their essences and emanations, their Logos and Demi-urgos, Aeons and Daemons male and female, with a long train of Etc. Etc. Etc. or, shall I say at once, of Nonsense.

The solution was to separate the *sayings* of Jesus, at least those that seem in accordance with what we can glean of his character, from the miraculous *doings* ascribed to him by the apostles. This Jefferson did for himself, literally taking a razor to the New Testament and excising everything that seemed to him dubious.

> I have performed this operation for my own use, by cutting verse by verse out of the printed book, and arranging, the matter which is evidently his, and which is as easily distinguishable as diamonds in a dunghill. The result is an 8vo. [octavo] of 46. pages of pure and unsophisticated doctrines, such as were professed and acted upon by the *unlettered* apostles, the Apostolic fathers, and the Christians of the 1st. century.

Indeed he had done it twice: first in 1804, creating a document he called "The Philosophy of Jesus," and then again, far more extensively, in 1820. This final work, "The Life and Morals of Jesus of Nazareth Extracted Textually from the Gospels," remained unpublished until 1903, when it was printed by the U.S. Congress for perusal by its members, and since that time it has enjoyed considerable popularity among agnostics and freethinkers. Needless to say, Jefferson himself was cagey about these activities of his, confiding only in trusted and like-minded friends such as Adams, Priestley, and Rush. It was his lifelong policy, reinforced by bitter experience in the political arena, to keep his unorthodox religious notions to himself.

Jefferson wrote of Priestley: "I have read his Corruptions of Christianity, and Early opinions of Jesus, over and over again; and I rest on them, and on [Conyers] Middleton's writings, especially his letters from Rome, and to Waterland, as the basis of my own faith." Priestley, as is described in Chapter Eight, espoused a simple system of ethics as preached by Jesus, and denounced subsequent corruptions; Middleton (1683–1750), an English divine, spoke out against all biblical miracles and mysteries. What Jefferson called his "faith," then, was indistinguishable from what most of us would define as ethics, informed by reason. Faith for faith's sake, the leap of faith that has been so important in Christian thought, meant nothing to him: he himself defined belief, religious and otherwise, as "the assent of the mind to an intelligible proposition." Much, far too much, of Christian dogma he considered the very opposite of intelligible.

Jefferson's lifelong hatred of the clergy applied equally to every sect and creed, and verged on the paranoic. He seemed to see every single Christian priest and minister throughout history as having been involved in some vast right-wing conspiracy. "The Christian priesthood, finding the doctrines of Christ levelled to every understanding, and too plain to need explanation, saw, in the mysticisms of Plato, materials with which they might build up an artificial system which might, from it's indistinctness, admit everlasting controversy, give employment for their order, and introduce it to profit, power and pre-eminence," he claimed. The exploitation of mysticism and magic, he assured his friends, "constitutes the power and the profits of the priests. Sweep away their gossamer fabrics of factitious religion, and they would catch no more flies." He insisted that "the mountebanks calling themselves the priests of Jesus" were able to flourish only by obscuring simple truth with mumbo jumbo: if their nonsensical doctrines could be understood, "it would not answer their purpose. Their security is in their faculty of shedding darkness, like the scuttle-fish, thro' the element in which they move, and making it impenetrable to the eye of a pursuing enemy."

As a democrat with distinctly radical, Jacobin leanings (he openly supported the extremists during the French Revolution), Jefferson automatically disapproved of the priesthood as a hierarchical and tradition-bound institution. As an amateur scientist and Enlightenment intellectual, he despised its resistence to science and reason. Priests, he wrote, "dread the advance of science as witches do the approach of day-light." This cry, incidentally, would be echoed by H. L. Mencken more than a century later: "every priest who really understands the nature of his business is well aware that science is its natural and implacable enemy." Mencken was writing within the context of the 1925 Scopes Trial which pitted Creationists against the expounders of evolution. We, in the twenty-first century, are replaying the old drama with our own concerns: not only evolution *versus* "intelligent design" this time, but stem-cell research and other bioethical issues. Can there be any doubt which side of the debate Jefferson would take?

All priests were bad, in Jefferson's view, but the Presbyterians were the worst of the lot.

The Presbyterian clergy are the loudest, the most intolerant of all sects; the most tyrannical and ambitious, ready at the word of the law-giver, if such a word could now be obtained, to put their torch to the pile, and to rekindle in this virgin hemisphere the flame in which their oracle, Calvin, consumed the poor Servetus, because he could not subscribe to the proposition of Calvin, that magistrates have a right to exterminate all heretics to the Calvinistic creed! They pant to re-establish by law that holy inquisition which they can now only infuse into public opinion.

His native Virginia he believed to be a fairly tolerant state, but this was not true, he claimed, "in the districts where Presbyterianism prevails undividedly. Their ambition and tyranny would tolerate no rival if they had power. Systematical in grasping at an ascendancy over all other sects, they aim, like the Jesuits, at engrossing the education of the country, are hostile to every institution they do not direct, and jealous at seeing others begin to attend at all to that object." And he was overjoyed when in 1817 the diehard Calvinistic state of Connecticut elected as governor the liberal Oliver Wolcott, who would finally disestablish the powerful Congregational church in that state, following the example Jefferson had set more than thirty years earlier with his Virginia Statute for Religious Freedom. Connecticut, Jefferson said, had been resurrected to "light and liberality," and he rejoiced that "this den of the priesthood is at length broken up, and that a protestant popedom is no longer to disgrace the American history and character." Adams did not share his optimism on this subject, and reminded his friend that the Calvinist denizens of New England and elsewhere would "whip and crop, pillory and roast" if they could. But in the event, ironically, New England soon did become theologically more liberal while Jefferson's tolerant Virginia and its neighboring Southern states would succumb to a neo-Calvinist fundamentalism that has proved to be, if not a Protestant popedom, then certainly what Jefferson—and Adams—would have considered a disgrace to the American history and character.

As with other Enlightenment gentlemen such as George Washington, Jefferson seems really to have been more concerned with philosophical than with religious ideals, in particular the principles of Stoicism and Epicureanism. "I too am an Epicurian," he wrote to his friend William Short. "I consider the genuine (not the imputed) doctrines of Epicurus as containing everything rational in moral philosophy which Greece and Rome have left us. Epictetus, indeed, has given us what was good of the Stoics . . ." An extremely telling missive of 1821 expresses Jefferson's hope "that the human mind will some day get back to the freedom it enjoyed 2000 years ago. This country, which has given the world an example of physical liberty, owes to it that of moral emancipation also." To express the belief that intellectual freedom had reached a height during ancient times that it had never again equaled was an implicit attack on Christianity, the mental system that replaced classical philosophy: Edward Gibbon's ferociously anti-Christian *Decline and Fall of the Roman Empire*, written during Jefferson's youth, was the most famous book expounding this theory, and nothing in Jefferson's voluminous writings would lead one to think that his own views diverged in any way from Gibbon's.

Believing, as he did, that Reason and Nature are the only revelation we have been given, Jefferson, perhaps inevitably, regarded the moral sense as natural, springing not from the external laws imposed by religion—the Ten Commandments, the Torah, or any other system—but from each human being's own inner sense of what is *naturally* right and just. The moral sense, he wrote, was "instinct, and innate."

[N]ature hath implanted in our breasts a love of others, a sense of duty to them, a moral instinct, in short, which prompts us irresistibly to feel and to succor their distresses. . . . It is true that they are not planted in every man, because there is no rule without exceptions; but it is false reasoning which converts exceptions into the general rule. Some men were born without the organs of sight, or of hearing, or without hands. Yet it would be wrong to say that man is born without those faculties, and sight, hearing, and hands may with truth enter into the general definition of man.

Jefferson insisted that this moral code existed *independently* of religious beliefs. "If we did a good act merely from the love of God and a belief that it is pleasing to him," he asked, "whence arises the morality of the Atheist? It is idle to say, as some do, that no such being exists."

Jefferson's moral and political philosophy as outlined above shaped his career, and in the process did much to shape the new nation he did so much to bring into the world. The tone he set, the political and philosophical tenor, cannot be overestimated, and in no department was this more true than in the separation of church and state, a radical and unprecedented proposition at the time of the nation's founding.

The concept of religious freedom was a lifelong obsession of Jefferson's. While Locke had advocated mere "toleration"—that is, an established religion with other faiths legally tolerated—Jefferson strongly fought for universal freedom of religion with no established sect at all. His first drafts of the Virginia Constitution, written during the early months of 1776, specify that "All persons shall have full and free liberty of religious opinion; nor shall any be compelled to frequent or maintain any religious institution." Later that year he perused the political writings of Locke and Shaftesbury in an attempt to apply their ideas, so far as it was possible, to the American scene. His private notes on the subject are quite revealing. Here are some selections:

> Our Saviour chose not to propagate his religion by temporal pun[ish]m[en]ts or civil incapacitations, if he had it was in his almighty power. But he chose [to] extend it by it's influence on reason, thereby shewing to others how [they] should proceed.

The life & essence of religion consists in the internal
persuasion of belief of the mind. External forms [of wor]ship,
when against our belief, are hypocrisy [and im]piety.

If any man err from the right way, it is his own misfortune , no
injury to thee, nor therefore art thou to punish him in the
things of this life because thou supposest he will be miserable
in that which is to come. On the contrary acc[or]d[in]g to the
spirit of the gospel, charity, bounty, liberality is due to him.

No man complains of his neighbor for ill management of his
affairs, for an error in sowing his land, or marrying his
daughter, for consuming his substance in taverns, pulling
down, build &c. In all these he has his liberty: but if he do not
frequent the church, or there conform to ceremonies, there is
an immediate uproar.

Locke denies toleration to those who entertain op[inio]ns
contrary to those moral rules necessary for the preservation of
society. . . . *But where he stopped short, we may go on* [italics
mine].

If magistracy should vouchsafe to interpose thus in other
sciences we should [have] as bad logic, mathematics &
philosophy as we have divinity in countries where the law
settles orthodoxy.

"Where he [Locke] stopped short, we may go on." Jefferson meant
that where Locke endorsed only toleration—toleration for dissenters
from an established church—the new United States should go further and endorse full religious freedom for all: an unprecedented experiment. Work that Jefferson would do later that year as a delegate
to the Continental Congress included writing the rough draft of the
Resolutions for Disestablishing the Church of England and for Repealing Laws Interfering with Freedom or Worship, and a draft of a

Bill Exempting Dissenters from Contributing to the Support of the Church.

Jefferson served as governor of Virginia from 1779 to 1781. The Anglican church had been disestablished there during the Revolution, but full religious liberty had not been achieved, and this disagreeable fact remained a thorn in Jefferson's side. He derided the "religious slavery, under which a people have been willing to remain, who have lavished their lives and fortunes for the establishment of their civil freedom." *Notes on the State of Virginia*, which he wrote in 1781–1782, contains passionate diatribes on this subject, among which the most famous is the following passage:

> Reason and experiment have been indulged, and error has fled before them. It is error alone which needs the support of government. Truth can stand by itself. Subject opinion to coercion: whom will you make your inquisitors? Fallible men; men governed by bad passions, by private as well as public reasons. And why subject it to coercion? To produce uniformity. But is uniformity of opinion desirable? No more than of face and stature. Introduce the bed of Procrustes then, and as there is danger that the large men may beat the small, make us all of a size, by lopping the former and stretching the latter. Difference of opinion is advantageous in religion. The several sects perform the office of a Censor morum over each other. Is uniformity attainable? Millions of innocent men, women, and children, since the introduction of Christianity, have been burnt, tortured, fined, imprisoned; yet we have not advanced one inch towards uniformity.
>
> What has been the effect of coercion? To make one half the world fools, the other half hypocrites. To support roguery and error all over the earth. Let us reflect that it is inhabited by a thousand different systems of religion. That ours is but one of that thousand. That if there be but one right, and ours that

one, we should wish to see the 999 wandering sects gathered
into the fold of truth. But against such a majority we cannot
effect this by force.

Could there be more potent evidence that Jefferson was what our
own contemporaries would call a religious relativist, and a liberal hu-
manist *par exellence*? *Notes on the State of Virginia* created a sensation
in the salons of Paris when it was published there in 1785, raising its
author's already high reputation in those circles.

Despite the fact that there was no established church in Virginia,
a number of its prominent men, led by the religiously conservative
Patrick Henry, believed that citizens of the state should pay a tax to
support all churches there. Madison spearheaded the resistance to
Henry's proposed Bill for a Religious Assessment, and Jefferson
egged him on from France, where he was serving as American minister. Then, in 1786, Madison steered through the Virginia legislature the Virginia Statute for Religious Freedom, which Jefferson had
composed nearly a decade before. This document, which remains in
the Virginia constitution, would become the basis for the Religious
Clauses in the Bill of Rights three years later. Written in the same
ringing prose that etched the Declaration of Independence on the
nation's collective memory, it deserves to be quoted in full. (The italics in paragraphs I and III are mine.)

> I. WHEREAS Almighty God hath created the mind free; that all
> attempts to influence it by temporal punishments or burthens,
> or by civil incapacitations, tend only to beget habits of
> hypocrisy and meanness, and are a departure from the plan of
> the Holy author of our religion, who being Lord both of body
> and mind, yet chose not to propagate it by coercions on either,
> as was in his Almighty power to do; that the impious
> presumptions of legislators and rulers, civil as well as
> ecclesiastical, who being themselves but fallible and uninspired
> men, have assumed dominion over the faith of others, hath

established and maintainted false religions over the greatest part of the world, and through all time; that to compel a man to furnish contributions of money for the propagation of opinions which he disbelieves, is sinful and tyrannical; that even the forcing him to support this or that teacher of his own religious persuasion, is depriving him of the comfortable liberty of giving his contributions to the particular pastor, whose morals he would make his pattern, and whose powers he feels most persuasive to righteousness, and is withdrawing from the ministry those temporary rewards, which proceeding from an approbation of their personal conduct, are an additional incitement to earnest and unremitting labours for the instruction of mankind; that our civil rights have no dependence on our religious opinions, any more than our opinions in physics and geometry; that therefore the proscribing any citizen as unworthy the public confidence by laying upon him an incapacity of being called to offices of trust and emolument, unless he profess or renounce this or that religious opinion, is depriving him injuriously of those privileges and advantages to which in common with his fellow-citizens he has a natural right; that it tends only to corrupt the principles of that religion it is meant to encourage, by bribing with a monopoly of wor[l]dly honours and emoluments, those who will externally profess and conform to it; that though indeed these are criminal who do not withstand such temptation, yet neither are those innocent who lay the bait in their way; that to suffer the civil magistrate to intrude his powers into the field of opinion, and to restrain the profession or propagation of principles on supposition of their ill tendency, is a dangerous fallacy, which at once destroys all religious liberty, because he being of course judge of that tendency will make his opinions the rule of judgment; and approve or condemn the sentiments of others only as they shall square with or differ from his own; that it is time enough for the rightful purposes of civil government, for its officers to interfere when principles break out into overt acts against peace and good order; and finally, that *truth is great and will prevail if left to herself, that she is the proper and sufficient antagonist to error, and has nothing to fear from the conflict, unless by human interposition disarmed of her natural weapons, free argument and debate, errors ceasing to be dangerous when it is permitted freely to contradict them.*

II. *Be it enacted by the General Assembly,* That no man shall be compelled to frequent or support any religious worship, place, or ministry whatsoever, nor shall be enforced restrained, molested, or burthened in his body or goods, nor shall otherwise suffer on account of his religious opinions or belief; but that all men shall be free to profess, and by argument to maintain, their opinion in matters of religion, and that the same shall in no wise diminish, enlarge, or affect their civil capacities.

III. And though we well know that this assembly elected by the people for the ordinary purposes of legislation only, have no power to restrain the acts of succeeding assemblies, constituted with powers equal to our own, and that therefore to declare this act to be irrevocable would be of no effect in law; yet *we are free to declare, and do declare, that the rights hereby asserted are of the natural rights of mankind,* and that if any act shall be hereafter passed to repeal the present, or to narrow its operation such act will be an infringement of natural right.

A note about "the Holy author of our religion," in paragraph I: some of the legislators proposed that the name "Jesus Christ" be inserted before this phrase. This insertion, Jefferson recounted in his biography with considerable satisfaction, "was rejected by a great majority, in proof that they meant to comprehend, within the mantle of its protection, the Jew and the Gentile, the Christian and Mahometan, the Hindoo, and Infidel of every denomination." Jefferson was unusual, in his time as in our own, in specifying his respect for the rights of the "infidel."

The author of this document was understandably proud—so much so that he requested that this achievement be etched on his tombstone, along with two others: his authorship of the Declaration of Independence and his founding of the University of Virginia. When the *Statute* was printed in Europe it was received, as Jefferson pointed out complacently, "with infinite approbation," and was even inserted into the new *Encyclopédie*. "In fact it is comfortable," he commented to Madison, "to see the standard of reason at length erected, after so many ages during which the human mind has been held in vassalage by kings, priests, and nobles: and it is honorable for us to have produced the first legislature who has had the courage to declare that the reason of man may be trusted with the formation of his own opinions."

Jefferson was absent in France during the Constitutional Convention, but he kept in close touch with the proceedings through his correspondence with Madison, the chief architect of the Constitution. Jefferson vigorously advocated a Bill of Rights, which not all the delegates were persuaded was necessary. He was also influential in spreading the ideals of the American Bill of Rights to France, for while there he helped the Marquis de Lafayette draft a French charter of rights that would become the basis for the Declaration of Rights that Lafayette presented to the National Assembly at Versailles in July 1789.

Jefferson served as secretary of state under Washington and vice president under Adams, during which time his reputation as an atheist and a rank democrat grew apace. ("Oh Lord!" intoned a Connecticut minister in the midst of a prayer for the welfare of President-elect Adams: "Wilt Thou bestow upon the Vice President a double

portion of Thy grace, for *Thou knowest he needs it*.") Conversation at
the Virginia Voltaire's dinner table could shock even his friends. The
portraitist John Trumbull, for example, here describes an evening at
Jefferson's home in 1793 at which Senator Giles of Virginia

> proceeded so far at last, as to ridicule the character, conduct
> and doctrines of the divine founder of our religion—
> Jefferson, in the mean time, smiling and nodding approbation
> on Mr. Giles, while the rest of the company silently left me
> and my defense to our fate; until at length my friend, David
> Franks, (first cashier of the Bank of the United States,) took
> up the argument on my side. Thinking this a fair opportunity
> for evading further conversation on this subject, I turned to
> Mr. Jefferson and said, "Sir, this is a strange situation in
> which I find myself; in a country professing Christianity, and
> at a table with Christians, as I supposed, I find my religion
> and myself attacked with severe and almost irresistible wit
> and raillery, and not a person to aid in my defense, but my
> friend Mr. Franks, *who is himself a Jew*." For a moment, this
> attempt to parry the discussion appeared to have some effect;
> but Giles soon returned to the attack, with new virulence, and
> burst out with—"It is all miserable delusion and priestcraft; I
> do not believe one word of all they say about a future state of
> existence, and retribution for actions done here. I do not
> believe one word of a Supreme Being who takes cognizance
> of the paltry affairs of this world, and to whom we are
> responsible for what we do." I had never before heard, or
> seen in writing, such a broad and unqualified avowal of
> atheism.

During the presidential election of 1800, which pitted Jefferson
against the incumbent Adams, religion became for the first time a
major campaign issue, establishing a destructive and divisive precedent. The following item, which was placed in the *Gazette of the*

United States several times monthly during the campaign, crudely announced the Federalist party line:

THE GRAND QUESTION STATED

At the present solemn and momentous epoch, the only question to be asked by every American, laying his hand on his heart, is "Shall I continue in allegiance to

GOD—AND A RELIGIOUS
PRESIDENT;

or impiously declare for
Jefferson—and no god!!!"

Anticipating the machinations of political manipulators like Ralph Reed and Karl Rove, Alexander Hamilton cynically played on the religious sentiments and prejudices of the American electorate to blacken the Republican candidate's character. Jefferson's long history as a freethinker had made him vulnerable as a candidate for national office, and Hamilton exploited this vulnerability by presenting Adams, the Federalist man, as especially pious. This dichotomy was as false as such political dichotomies usually are, for as we know Adams could hardly have been described as an orthodox Christian, nor was Hamilton himself, at that time, any more devout than Jefferson. But appearance is everything in politics, and Jefferson was widely perceived, in the words of the New England jurist Theophilus Parsons, as the "great arch priest of Jacobinism and infidelity." In a Jefferson presidency, the *Connecticut Courant* editorialized, "Murder, robbery, rape, adultery, and incest will all be openly taught and practiced."

But Jefferson turned out to be just as canny a politician as Hamilton. He managed to turn the negative campaigning of his opponents against them by representing them (as falsely as they had characterized him) as reactionary proponents of an established church; specifically, he exploited the hatred and fear of Presbyterians among the rapidly growing ranks of Baptists, Methodists, and other nonconforming sects, implying that the Federalists would seek to reverse the course of the nation's long battle for religious freedom.

This tactic might have been what won the election for Jefferson. Adams, at least, believed that to be the case. As he wrote to Mercy Warren some years later, "With the Baptists, Quakers, Methodists, and Moravians, as well as the Dutch and German Lutherans and Calvinists, it had an immense effect, and turned them in such numbers as decided the election. They said, let us have an Atheist or Deist or any thing rather than an establishment of Presbyterianism." Thomas Paine, observing the mood of the people in the months preceding the election, agreed with this judgment. "When I was in Connecticut . . . ," he recalled a few years later, "I fell in company with some Baptists among whom were three ministers. The conversation turned on the election for President, and one of them who appeared to be a leading man said, 'They cry out against Mr. Jefferson because they say he is a Deist. Well, a Deist may be a good man, and if he think it right, it is right to him. For my own part,' said he, 'I had rather vote for a Deist than for a blue-skin Presbyterian.'" In other words, better a *laissez-faire* president with little or no religion than a pious president intent on promoting his own sect.

As president, Jefferson took the federal doctine of church/state separation absolutely literally. He entirely refrained, for example, from proclaiming fasts and thanksgivings. Many objected. Jefferson laid out his considered reasons for this policy in his Second Inaugural Address, then later and more extensively in an 1808 letter to a clergyman friend, the Reverend Samuel Miller [the italics are mine]:

> I consider the government of the U.S. as interdicted by the constitution from intermeddling with religious institutions, their doctrines, discipline, or exercises. . . . But it is only

proposed that I should *recommend*, not prescribe a day of fasting & prayer. That is, that I should *indirectly* assume to the U.S. an authority over religious exercises which the Constitution has directly precluded them from. It must be meant too that this recommendation is to carry some authority, and to be sanctioned by some penalty on those who disregard it; not indeed of fine and imprisonment, but of some degree of proscription perhaps in public opinion. And does the change in the nature of the penalty make the recommendation the less a *law* of conduct for those to whom it is directed? *I do not believe it is for the interest of religion to invite the civil magistrate to direct it's exercises, it's discipline, or it's doctrines; nor of the religious societies that the general government should be invested with the power of effecting any uniformity of time or matter among them.* Fasting & prayer are religious exercises. The enjoining them an act of discipline. Every religious society has a right to determine for itself the times for these exercises, & the objects proper for them, according to their own particular tenets; and this right can never be safer than in their own hands, where the constitution has deposited it.

But Washington and Adams, critics pointed out, had proclaimed thanksgivings. Jefferson argued that this precedent should have no significance, and that the first two presidents' proclamations (which Jefferson gently implied were thoughtless mistakes) had probably been responsible for sanctioning the essentially illogical assumption that the federal government has *any right* to intervene in this area.

I am aware that the practice of my predecessors may be quoted. But I have ever believed that the example of state executives led to the assumption of that authority by the general government, without due examination, which would have discovered that what might be a right in a state government, was a violation of that right when assumed by another. Be this as it may, every one must act according to the dictates of his own reason, & mine tells me that *civil powers alone have been given to the President of the U.S. and no authority to direct the religious exercises of his constituents.*

During Jefferson's long retirement from public service, which lasted from 1809 until his death in 1826, his favorite project was the creation of the University of Virginia. The College of William and Mary, which he himself had attended and which had been Virginia's principal educational establishment from colonial times, he saw as retrograde, worn out, and philosophically nil: "just well enough endowed to draw out the miserable existence to which a miserable constitution has doomed it." As he described it in his autobiography,

> The College of William and Mary was an establishment purely of the Church of England; the Visitors were required to be all of that Church; the Professors to subscribe its thirty-nine articles; its Students to learn its Catechism; and one of its fundamental objects was declared to be, to raise up Ministers for that church.

The new university, on the contrary, would be created on a plan "so broad and liberal and *modern*, as to be worth patronizing with the public support, and be a temptation to the youth of other states to come and drink the cup of knowledge and fraternize with us."

Jefferson took the primary role in establishing the curriculum of the new university: those interested in the subject might consult his letter to Peter Carr of September 7, 1814, in which he laid out his ideas for the curriculum in great detail. He had many guiding principles, but of these the most important was that the university should act as a philosophical reflection of the Virginia Statue for Religious Freedom. He opposed the establishment of a chair of divinity, explaining his reasons for doing so in a Report of the Commissioners for the University of Virginia:

In conformity with the principles of our Constitution, which places all sects of religion on an equal footing, with the jealousies of the different sects in guarding that equality from encroachment and surprise, and with the sentiments of the legislature in favor of freedom of religion, manifested on former occasions, we have proposed no professor of divinity; and the rather as the proofs of the being of a God, the creator, preserver, and supreme ruler of the universe, the author of all the relations of morality, and of the laws and obligations these infer, will be within the province of the professor of ethics. . . .

Religion, in other words, was to be treated in ethical rather than doctrinal terms.

Not that Jefferson meant to banish all religious expression from his "Academical Village": rather, each denomination was allowed to take part on an exactly equal basis. Sectarian schools of divinity were invited to set up shop in the vicinity of the university so that their students might avail themselves of the educational offerings of this secular institution. Jefferson even attempted to extend this principle to Virginia's public elementary schools, proposing in 1817 a School Act that would exclude ministers of the gospel from acting as school trustees and bar religious instruction specific to any one sect or denomination; but this act was rejected by the Virginia legislature.

The Second Great Awakening, which had begun around 1799 and caused Jefferson so much trouble during his first presidential campaign, had accelerated by the time he retired. By then he was relieved of the political necessity of paying any sort of lip service to religion and its ministers, and he occasionally let blast with the full force of his disgust. Confidential letters to friends, now published and available for anyone to read, can leave us in no doubt as to his real opinions.

These reverend leaders of the Hartford nation [Presbyterian clergy of New England] it seems then are now falling together about religion, of which they have not one real principle in their hearts. Like bawds, religion becomes to them a refuge from the despair of their loathesome vices. They seek in it only an oblivion of the disgrace with which they have loaded themselves, in their political ravings, and of their mortification at the ridiculous issue of their Hartford convention. (Letter to Dr. Benjamin Waterhouse, October 13, 1815)

In our Richmond there is much fanaticism, but chiefly among the women. They have their nightly meetings and praying parties, where, attended by their priests, and sometimes by a hen-pecked husband, they pour forth the effusions of their love for Jesus, in terms as amatory and carnal, as their modesty would permit them to use to a mere earthly lover. (Letter to Dr. Thomas Cooper, November 2, 1822)

You judge truly that I am not afraid of the priests. They have tried upon me all their various batteries, of pious whining, hypocritical canting, lying and slandering, without being able to give me one moment of pain. I have contemplated their order from the Magi of the East to the Saints of the West, and I have found no difference in character, but of more or less caution, in proportion to their information or ignorance of those on whom their interested duperies were to be plaid off. Their sway in New England is indeed formidable. No mind beyond mediocrity dares there to develop itself. . . .

They are now looking to the flesh pots of the South and aiming at foothold there by their missionary teachers. They have lately come forward boldly with their plan to establish "a qualified religious instructor over every thousand souls in the US." And they seem to consider none as qualified but their own sect. (Letter to Horatio Gates Spafford, January 10, 1816)

Jefferson did not even go along with the argument, so frequently put forward by modern proponents of a Christian America, that our legal system is philosophically based on holy scripture. The principles of our Constitution are largely derived from English common law, and during Jefferson's lifetime the great English jurist Sir William Blackstone had asserted that common law was based on Christianity. Jefferson devoted a good hunk of time during his retirement to refuting that claim through his own scholarly research. Common law, he said, was originally a Saxon institution.

> For we know that the common law is that system of law which was introduced by the Saxons on their settlement in England, and altered from time to time by proper legislative authority from that time to the date of Magna Charta. . . . This settlement took place about the middle of the fifth century. But Christianity was not introduced till the seventh century; the conversion of the first christian king of the Heptarchy having taken place about the year 598, and that of the last about 686. Here, then, was a space of two hundred years, during which the common law was in existence, and Christianity no part of it. . . . If, therefore, from the settlement of the Saxons to the introduction of Christianity among them, that system of religion could not be a part of the common law, because they were not yet Christians, and if, having their laws from that period to the close of the common law, we are all able to find among them no such act of adoption, we may safely affirm (though contradicted by all the judges and writers on earth) that Christianity neither is, nor ever was a part of the common law.

Biblical authority was later introduced, as he proved ingeniously, by a "pious fraud," of which he gave detailed accounts in letters to friends.*

---

*Pertinent excerpts from Jefferson's letter to John Adams of January 24, 1814, and from him to John Cartright of June 5, 1824, may be read in Appendix I.

For modern anti-separationists to claim that Thomas Jefferson, of all people, was a good Christian who really didn't mean what we do by separation of church and state, smacks of desperation—just how flimsy is their case if it cannot stand without the support of the Virginia Voltaire, the arch-Jacobin? There are, certainly, Founding Fathers who were devout Christians: John Jay and Benjamin Rush, for example. But no one who has seriously looked into the question could ever pretend to claim Thomas Jefferson as one of their number. Arm in arm with his friend James Madison, Jefferson in fact tried harder than any other Founding Father to remove religion definitively from the political life of the new nation.

CHAPTER FIVE

Madison

"There is not a shadow of right in the general
government to intermeddle with religion.
Its least interference with it would be a
most flagrant usurpation."

—James Madison

☒ ALONG WITH JEFFERSON, no Founding Father was more vocal in the cause of separation of chuch and state, or more influential and effective in implementing this principle, than James Madison, the United States' fourth president. As leader of the opposition to religious assessments in the Virginia legislature and as author of the "Memorial and Remonstrance Against Religious Assessments," a classic document of Enlightenment political philosophy, as the chief architect of the U.S. Constitution and as principal author, with Alexander Hamilton, of the Federalist Papers, the magnificent apologia for that Constitution, the brilliant Madison, determined to the point of doggedness, did more than anyone to formulate the intellectual and philosophical principles that underlay the American Revolution and to transform them into a durable legal construction.

Madison's mental achievement was solid, monumental, considered. While Jefferson entertained the occasional crackpot idea and paranoid fantasy, Madison was always a model not only of intellectual integrity but of common sense, a rare commodity. His reflections on religious liberty, the wall of separation, and related matters are calm and thoughtful: no one could accuse him, as they might accuse Jefferson, of overstating his case with hysterical prejudice against the clergy. Yet the conclusions he drew, firmly grounded in their legal context, are more or less identical with Jefferson's.

Born in 1751, Madison came out of the same Virginia planter society as Washington and Jefferson. He initially studied at home with an Anglican minister of his family's church, but then chose to attend the Presbyterian Princeton (then called the College of New Jersey) rather than the Anglican William and Mary. There he came under the influence of the college's legendary president, John Witherspoon. Witherspoon was a Presbyterian minister who had come to America from Scotland in 1768, bringing with him the fresh liberal breezes of the Scottish Enlightenment. He espoused the principles of Common Sense philosophy, which stressed empiricism and advocated the testing of religious faith with reason and experience. His students read Locke, Montesquieu, Harrington, Grotius, Hobbes, and a wide variety of other seventeenth- and eighteenth-century philosophers. Witherspoon took seriously the college's stated mission of forming graduates who would be "ornaments of the State as well as the Church," and he himself would serve as a delegate to the Second Continental Congress. During his tenure at Princeton his students would include not only a future president, Madison, but a future vice president, nine cabinet officers, twenty-one senators, thirty-nine congressmen, three Supreme Court justices, and twelve state governors.

Madison had an earnest temperament. Like Adams, he was prudish and pious in early life, but as the years went on he became increasingly worldly and unshockable. Yet even in his youth he entertained very strong feelings about the indecency of religious coercion. "Religious bondage shackles and debilitates the mind and unfits it for every noble enterprize every expanded prospect," he opined as early as 1774. That same year he wrote to a friend that "Union of Religious Sentiments begets a surprizing confidence and Ecclesiastical Establishments tend to great ignorance and Corruption all of which facilitate the Execution of mischievous Projects. . . . That diabolical Hell conceived principle of persecution rages among some and to their eternal Infamy the Clergy can furnish their Quota of Imps for such business." At that time Madison was still conventionally religious, despite such violent rhetoric, but his orthodoxy would fade with age, and later in life his state of mind can only be described as agnostic:

> The finiteness of the human understanding betrays itself on all subjects, but more especially when it contemplates such as involve infinity. What may safely be said seems to be, that the infinity of time & space forces itself on our conception, a limitation of either being inconceivable; that the mind prefers at once the idea of a self-existing cause to that of an infinite series of cause & effect, which augments, instead of avoiding difficulty; and that it finds more facility in assenting to the self-existence of an invisible cause possessing infinite power, wisdom & goodness, than to the self-existence of the universe, visibly destitute of those attributes, and which may be the effect of them. In this comparative facility of conception & belief, all philosophical Reasoning on the subject must perhaps terminate.

Mankind finds it easier and more comfortable, that is, to believe in a god than not to—and that is the most that can be said on the subject.

Plagued by ill health, Madison very early abandoned any thought of a physically active life and gave himself over to serious study. His intensive reading in law, history, government, and political philosophy turned him into one of the most learned among his many learned friends and colleagues. Of the historical patterns he discerned during the course of his studies, one in particular would stamp itself on his consciousness: that "a zeal for different opinions concerning religion" has throughout history "inflamed [men and women] with mutual animosity, and rendered them much more disposed to vex and oppress each other, than co-operate for their common good."

As a delegate to Virginia's Revolutionary Convention in 1776, Madison was a member of the committee in charge of writing a "declaration of rights." George Mason was to be the author of the declaration, but Madison disagreed with Mason's wording and suggested an amendment. It is worth looking both at Mason's original statement and Madison's changes to gain an insight into the latter's thinking on the subject. Mason's original:

> That as Religion, or the Duty which we owe to our divine and omnipresent Creator, and the Manner of discharging it, can be governed only by Reason and Conviction, not by Force or Violence; and therefore that all Men should enjoy the fullest Toleration in the Exercise of Religion, according to the Dictates of Conscience, unpunished and unrestrained by the Magistrate, unless, under Colour of Religion, any Man disturb the Peace, the Happiness, or Safety of Society, or of Individuals. And that it is the mutual Duty of all, to practice Christian Forbearance, Love and Charity towards Each other.

And Madison's amendment:

> That Religion or the duty we owe to our Creator, and the manner of discharging it, being under the direction of reason and conviction only, not of violence or compulsion, all men are equally entitled to the full and free exercise of it accord[in]g to the dictates of Conscience; and therefore that no man or class

of men ought, on account of religion to be invested with peculiar emoluments or privileges; nor subjected to any penalties or disabilities unless under &c.

Madison's omissions are certainly significant: he rejected Mason's word "Toleration" as a loaded term (as we have seen, "toleration" did not amount to full religious liberty), and also Mason's reference to "Christian" virtues, seeking, probably, to include non-Christians in his concept of community. He also made the important point that citizens should be neither penalized nor rewarded on account of their religion. This last item was too much for the committee to swallow, and it didn't make it into the final draft. The troubling word "Christian" was also snuck back in. But Madison succeeded, at least, in getting rid of the always unsatisfactory "toleration."

During the Revolutionary War Madison served first in the Virginia Council of State—that is, as a member of the governor's cabinet—then as a delegate to the Continental Congress. His term there coming to an end in 1783, he returned to Virginia where he continued to lobby for religious freedom in the state assembly as the state's new constitution was drafted and debated.

Since 1776 the Virginia advocates for religious establishment had encountered serious opposition and accordingly shifted from endorsing the financial support of the Episcopal church in particular to the general financial support of all "Teachers of the Christian Religion." As the disapproving Madison expressed it in his own recollections many years later, "During the session of the General Assembly 1784–1785 a bill was introduced into the House of Delegates providing for the legal support of Teachers of the Christian Religion, and being patronized by the most popular talents in the House, seemed likely to obtain a majority of votes." If this were to pass, a tax, or assessment, would be levied on the people of Virginia to support these Christian ministers. The party in favor of the bill was led by Patrick Henry, while a significant and vocal opposition was spearheaded by

George Mason and Madison. In Madison's words, ". . . Col. Geo. Mason, Col. Geo. Nicholas also possessing much weight and some others thought it advisable that a remonstrance against the bill should be prepared for general circulation and signature and imposed on me the task of drawing up such a paper."

The lines were drawn, with the conservative Henry on one side and the separationists, Mason and Madison, on the other. Jefferson, who left to take up his ministerial position in France in mid-1784, kept in close contact with the proceedings through Madison's letters and contributed to its outcome through the advice he proferred and the great influence he had always wielded over the younger man.

Everything Madison saw served to remind him of the liberties church and clergy took whenever they were given the opportunity. In 1784 he wrote to Jefferson:

> The Episcopal Clergy introduced a notable project for re-establishing their independence of the laity. The foundation of it was that the whole body should be legally incorporated, invested with the present property of the Church, made capable of acquiring indefinitely—empowered to make canons & vestries to be immovable otherwise then by sentence of the Convocation. Extraordinary as such a project was, it was preserved from a dishonorable death by the talents of Mr. Henry. It lies over for another Session.

Jefferson's response was caustic.

> While Mr. Henry lives another bad constitution would be formed, & saddled for ever on us. What we have to do I think is devoutly pray for his death, in the mean time to keep alive the idea that the present is but an ordinance & to prepare the minds of the young men. I am glad the Episcopalians have again shewn their teeth & fangs. The dissenters had almost forgotten them.

He was pleased, in other words, that the Episcopalians were demonstrating just how dangerous they were, how ready to pull rank over the other sects, for he counted on the dissenters—Baptists, Methodists, Quakers, and others—to oppose religious assessments on the grounds that the chief beneficiaries would be the hated Episcopalians. In this he and Madison consciously played the populist card. Madison spelled this out quite explicitly in a subsequent letter to Jefferson.

> The opposition to the general assessment gains ground. . . .
> The presbyterian clergy have at length espoused the side of the
> opposition, being moved either by a fear of their laity or a
> jealousy of the episcopalians. The mutual hatred of these sects
> has been much inflamed by the late act incorporating the latter.
> I am far from being sorry for it as a coalition between them
> could alone endanger our religious rights and a tendency to
> such an event had been suspected.

Madison's policy, when dealing with different varieties of Christians, was to divide and rule; any real degree of political cooperation between the various sects would give them an inordinate amount of power, as later presidents and legislators have discovered, often to their dismay.

Madison kept a close eye on the preliminary skirmishes leading up to the fight over assessment. The following letter, written to James Monroe in 1785, shows just how disturbing he found the encroachment of religion on government to be. His words are of the greatest interest and pertinence in the modern battle over church/ state separation:

> It gives me much pleasure to observe by 2 printed reports sent
> me by Col. Grayson that in the latter Cong[res]s. had
> expunged a clause contained in the first for setting apart a
> district of land in each Township, for supporting the Religion
> of the Majority of inhabitants. How a regulation, so unjust in

itself, so foreign to the authority of Cong[res]s. so hurtful to the sale of public land, and smelling so strongly of an antiquated Bigotry, could have received the countenance of a Comm[it]tee is truly a matter of astonishment.

It is the old problem of the dictatorship of the majority, a question of great concern for those, whether on the right or the left, of libertarian leanings—as both Jefferson and Madison were. They believed that the fact that a majority of the people in a given community might be Episcopalian (or Baptist, or Congregationalist) was no justification for asking those of a different denomination or religion to contribute to the Episcopalian (or Baptist, or Congregational) church.

The entire text of Madison's 1785 "Memorial and Remonstrance Against Religious Assessments" is reprinted in Appendix II. In its preamble Madison attacked the proposed bill as "a dangerous abuse of power" and went on to list the reasonings of the party opposing it. In this document we find some of the strongest language he would ever use, marshaled for the purpose of a passionate defense of the principles of church/state separation. "[I]n matters of Religion," he wrote, "no mans right is abridged by the institution of Civil Society and that Religion is wholly exempt from its cognizance. True it is, that no other rule exists, by which any question may divide a Society, can be ultimately determined, but the will of the majority; but it is also true that the majority may trespass on the rights of the minority." Here again we encounter the Madisonian concern for individual rights when they are threatened by majority tyranny.

In Article 3 of the "Memorial and Remonstrance," Madison addressed a problem that is still very much with us today. "[I]t is proper," he wrote, "to take alarm at the first experiment on our liberties." The importance of this principle, he went on, could hardly be exaggerated. "Who does not see that the same authority which can establish Christianity, in exclusion of all other Religions, may establish with the same ease any particular sect of Christians, in exclusion of all other Sects?" Therefore Madison did not believe that America should define itself as a Christian nation, even though the majority of its citizens might be practicing Christians, and he warned his fellow citizens about the dangers of allowing not just one particular sect but "Christianity" in its widest interpretation to be claimed as the national religion.

Freedom of religion Madison pronounced to be an "unalienable" right, and in any case, if such freedom should be abused it would be "an offense against God, not against man: To God, therefore, not to man, must an account of it be rendered." This statement is tantamount to an admission that the people's religion, or lack of it, is immaterial to the well-being of state and community.

In any case, Madison asked, what have been the results of state-sanctioned churches throughout the ages? "What influence in fact have ecclesiastical establishments had on Civil Society? In some instances they have been seen to erect a spiritual tyranny on the ruins of the Civil authority; in many instances they have been seen upholding the thrones of political tyranny: in no instance have they been seen the guardians of the liberties of the people." The history of the Christian church's alliance with power, he pointed out, had not been a pretty one. "During almost fifteen centuries has the legal establishment of Christianity been on trial," he said. "What have been its fruits? More or less in all places, pride and indolence in the Clergy, ignorance and servility in the laity, in both, superstition, bigotry and persecution."

These are strong words indeed. It is interesting to reflect that they came not from a newspaper editorialist or a student radical but from a leading legislator and politician. Would any such highly visible elected official get away with this sort of rhetoric today? One really doubts it. The following statement, too, is quite incendiary:

> Because the Bill implies either that the Civil Magistrate is a competent Judge of Religious Truth; or that he may employy

Religion as an engine of Civil policy. The first is an arrogant pretension falsified by the contradictory opinions of Rulers in all ages, and throughout the world: the second an unhallowed perversion of the means of salvation.

These are words that every politician who claims the authority or blessings of God should read, and remember. Madison, the father of the Constitution, was of the firm opinion that there is no reason we should accept civil magistrates as competent judges of religious truth.

The "Memorial and Remonstrance" succeeded beautifully: when the legislature assembled, "the number of Copies & signatures prescribed displayed such an overwhelming opposition of the people, that the proposed plan of a gen[era]l assessm[en]t was crushed under it. . . ." This clear victory provided Madison and his allies with all the momentum necessary to carry the Virginia Statute for Religious Freedom cleanly through the legislature the following year. "The enacting clauses past without a single alteration," he wrote after the statute's passage, "and I flatter myself [to] have in this Country extinguished for ever the ambitious hope of making laws for the human mind."

That same year, 1786, Madison and Alexander Hamilton were the leaders of the movement to amend the Articles of Confederation, which were proving an inadequate legal structure for a growing nation. The conference they endorsed eventually became the Constitutional Convention, of which Madison was to be the single most effective and influential member.

Throughout the months of often heated horse-trading that led to the creation of the United States Constitution, Madison was ceaselessly vigilant in the cause of religious freedom, and always mindful of the damage wrought by its suppression. Aware of the inadequacy of mere "toleration," he was eager to impose a religious settlement similar to that which had already been achieved in Virginia. Religious liberty ought to be defined, he said, "as distinctly as words can admit, and the limits to this authority [religious laws] established with as much solemnity as the forms of legislation express. . . . Every provision for them [laws] short of this principle, will be found to leave crevices at least through which bigotry may introduce persecution; a monster feeding and thriving on its own venom, gradually swells to a size and strength overwhelming all laws human and divine."

"Religion and government will both exist in greater purity, the less they are mixed together." This was Madison's public philosophy on the subject in a nutshell, and the Constitution in its final form reflects it. The original Constitution, without the Bill of Rights that would be added six months later, contains only one mention of religion: the injunction that "no religious test shall ever be required as a qualification to any office or public trust under the United States." While this seems mild enough now, it amounted to a radical innovation in its day, for Great Britain had traditionally required anyone who sought public office to profess allegiance to the Church of England—thereby effectively keeping Catholics and dissenters out of power—and several of the various state constitutions contained similar laws.

The "no religious test" clause was vigorously advocated by Madison. Any further mention of religion—as, for example, in the Bill of Rights which Jefferson and others were urging on the Convention—he resisted. Madison felt that a Bill of Rights, in specifying certain rights, would somehow imply that those rights were not obvious and "unalienable," and therefore would allow their foes to challenge their validity. Already, according to the existing Constitution, he felt that "There is not a shadow of right in the general government to intermeddle with religion. Its least interference with it would be a most flagrant usurpation." Also, "I am sure that the rights of Conscience in particular, if submitted to public definition would be narrowed much more than they are likely ever to be by an assumed power," he wrote to Jefferson in a considered statement of his reasons for thinking a Bill of

Rights unnecessary and even undesirable. He was of course overruled in this department, but he submitted with his characteristic grace and dignity to the proposed First Amendment, which formally provided among other rights that "Congress shall make no law respecting an establishment of religion, or prohibiting the free exercise thereof."

Madison in any case held the Enlightenment view of religion as more often a divisive than a uniting force, and felt that it should be treated with the utmost caution. So far from fostering virtue or restraint, it too often encouraged their exact opposites.

> Religion. The inefficacy of this restraint on individuals is well known. The conduct of every popular Assembly, acting on oath, the strongest of religious ties, shows that individuals join without remorse in acts ag[ain]st which their consciences would revolt, if proposed to them separately in their closets. When Indeed Religion is kindled into enthusiasm, its force like that of other passions is increased by the sympathy of a multitude. But enthusiasm is only a temporary state of Religion, and whilst it lasts will hardly be seen with pleasure at the helm. Even in its coolest state, it has been much oftener a motive to oppression than a restraint from it.

During his two-term presidency (1809–1817) Madison did not always feel empowered to act on the legal principles he advocated. He proclaimed, for example, several days of thanksgiving or prayer (which Jefferson, his predecessor in office, had staunchly refused to do). In 1814 when British armies burned the White House and Madison had to flee, he issued a proclamation of a day of public humiliation and fasting and of "prayer to Almighty God." As he later claimed in a sheaf of private notes (published for the first time in 1946 under the title "Detached Memoranda"), Madison did this under some constraint: he would rather have followed Jefferson's uncompromising example. "It was thought not proper to refuse a compliance altogether," he said about his own case; "but a form &

language were employed, which were meant to deaden as much as possible any claim of political right to enjoin religious observances by resting these expressly on the voluntary compliance of individuals. . . ." Madison's own preference, reinforced by years of legal studies and reflection, would have been to omit such proclamations as implying "a religious agency, making no part of the trust delegated to political rulers." Such proclamations, he said,

> seem to imply and certainly nourish the erronious idea of a national religion. The idea just as it related to the Jewish nation under a theocracy, having been improperly adopted by so many nations which have embraced Xnity, is too apt to lurk in the bosoms even of Americans, who in general are aware of the distinction between religious & political societies.

The key phrase is "the erronious idea of a national religion." To Madison, the chief architect of our Constitution, there had never been any such thing.

Oaths with a religious foundation, such as those sworn on the Bible, Madison found equally unconstitutional.

> Is not a religious test as far as it is necessary, or would operate, involved in the oath itself? If the person swearing believes in the supreme Being who is invoked, and in the penal consequences of offending him, either in this or a future world or both, he will be under the same restraint from perjury as if he had previously subscribed a test requiring this belief. If the person in question be an unbeliever in these points and would notwithstanding take the oath, a previous test could have no effect. He would subscribe it as he would take the oath, without any principle that could be affected by either.

The issue of the appointments of chaplains to Congress and to the armed forces was another subject on which Madison's actions while in office conflicted, to his lasting personal dissatisfaction, with his beliefs.

The current anti-separationist line, voiced here by Supreme Court Chief Justice Warren Burger, has been that "Clearly the men who wrote the First Amendment Religion Clauses did not view paid legislative chaplains and opening prayers as a violation of that Amendment, for the practice of opening sessions with prayer has continued without interruption ever since that early session of Congress." In fact this is very far from clear. What is clear is that Burger had not read, or had not remembered, Madison's "Detached Memoranda." In fact Madison's opinion on the subject was uncompromising: "The establishment of the chaplainship to Congress is a palpable violation of equal rights, as well as of Constitutional principles."

> The Constitution of the U.S. forbids everything like an establishment of a national religion. The law appointing Chaplains establishes a religious worship for the national representatives, to be performed by Ministers of religion, elected by a majority of them; and these are to be paid out of the national taxes. Does not this involve the principle of a national establishment, applicable to a provision for a religious worship for the Constitution as well as of the representative Body, approved by the majority, and conducted by Ministers of religion paid by the entire nation?

In any case, as he wrote privately to a friend, "it was not with my approbation, that the deviation from it took place in Cong[ress] when they appointed Chaplains, to be paid from the Nat[iona]l Treasury."

According to the Constitution and natural law, religion is purely a private matter; to require citizens to contribute financially to the salary of a minister of religion, whether or not they wish to do so, is clearly unconstitutional, Madison insisted.

> If Religion consist in voluntary acts of individuals, singly, or voluntarily associated, and it be proper that Public functionaries, as well as their Constituents should discharge

their religious duties, let them like their Constituents, do so at
their own expense. How small a contribution from each
member of Cong[ress] w[oul]d suffice for the purpose! How
just w[oul]d it be in its principle! How noble in its exemplary
sacrifice to the genius of the Constitution; and the divine right
of conscience! Why should the expense of a religious worship
be allowed for the Legislature, be paid by the public, more
than that for the Ex[ecutive] or Judiciary branch of the
Gov[ernment].

As for extending the institution of the chaplaincy into the armed
forces, Madison saw no more validity for it there than he did in Congress, and possibly less. As a firm republican and student of history
he knew that a pious army, after all, is likely to be a pliable one, a
more tractable instrument of tyrannical government.

Better also to disarm in the same way, the precedent of
Chaplainships for the army and navy, than erect them into a
political authority in matters of religion. . . . Look thro' the
armies & navies of the world, and say whether in the
appointment of their ministers of religion, the spiritual interest
of the flocks or the temporal interest of the Shepherds, be most
in view: whether here, as elsewhere the political care of religion
is not a nominal more than a real aid.

In any case the appointment of a chaplain would inevitably con-
stitute majority tyranny, a principle Madison always deplored.

Could a Catholic clergyman ever hope to be appointed
Chaplain? To say that his principles are obnoxious or that his
sect is small, is to lift the veil at once and exhibit in its native
deformity the doctrine that religious truth is to be tested by
numbers, or that the major sects have a right to govern the
minor.

The question of church property was one on which Madison was able to satisfactorily reconcile his principles with political exigencies during his presidency. Remembering that the enormous accumulation of property by the Catholic church and the abuses and corruption that devolved from this wealth had been instrumental in bringing about the wars and anarchy of the Reformation, Madison felt the need to warn his countrymen against legalizing such practices.

> But besides the danger of a direct mixture of Religion & civil Government, there is an evil which ought to be guarded ag[ain]st in the indefinite accumulation of property from the capacity of holding it in perpetuity by ecclesiastical corporations. The power of all corporations, ought to be limited in this respect. The growing wealth acquired by them never fails to be a source of abuses. . . . Are the U.S. duly awake to the tendency of the precedents they are establishing, in the multiplied incorporations of Religious Congregations with the faculty of acquiring & holding property real as well as personal?

In 1811 Madison brought these principles into play when he vetoed two bills, one incorporating an Episcopal church in the District of Columbia, and one reserving government land in the Mississippi territory for a Baptist church. The published veto for the Mississippi case states his position clearly:

> Because the bill in reserving a certain parcel of land of the United States for the use of said Baptist Church comprises a principle and precedent for the appropriation of funds of the United States for the use and support of religious societies, contrary to the article of the Constitution which declares that "Congress shall make no law respecting a religious establishment" [sic].

He objected to the District of Columbia bill on similar grounds, as well as others to do with the church's articles of incorporation. Furthermore—and this should be of the greatest interest today, with the debates over "faith-based" charities between the Bush administration and its critics—Madison objected even to the church's attempt to gain government sanction for its charitable activities.

> Because the Bill vests in the said incorporated Church, an authority to provide for the support of the poor, and the education of poor children of the same; an authority, which being altogether superfluous if the provision is to be the result of pious charity, would be a precedent [sic] for giving to religious Societies as such, a legal agency in carrying into effect a public and civil duty.

Madison, then, saw charity as "a public and civil duty," charity undertaken through religious societies as purely voluntary and private. This implies that he would have been an advocate of some form of public welfare system, and would have objected in no uncertain terms to taxpayer-supported "faith-based" charity efforts.

Madison, like Jefferson, devoted time during his years of retirement to planning and founding the University of Virginia. He shared Jefferson's determination to omit chairs of theology: as he wrote to Edward Everett, a Harvard professor, "A University with sectarian professorships, becomes, of course, a Sectarian Monopoly: with professorships of rival sects, it would be an Arena of Theological Gladiators. Without any such professorships it may incur for a time at least, the imputation of irreligious tendencies, if not designs. The last difficulty was thought [in setting up the University of Virginia] more manageable than either of the others."

The university was to be a state institution, endowed and supported at the common expense. Therefore any imposed theological program went by definition against the principles not only of the U.S. Constitution but of the Virginia Statute for Religious

Freedom, which had by then been incorporated into the state's constitution.

After he left the presidency in 1817, Madison had nearly two decades of rural retirement in which to reflect on the momentous events of the previous half-century and the part he had played in them. On the subject of religious freedom and church/state separation, his feelings never vacillated: these things, so far as he could see, had been uniformly and visibly beneficial. In a letter of 1821, for instance, he stated that "The experience of the United States is a happy disproof of the error so long rooted in the unenlightened minds of well-meaning Christians, as well as in the corrupt hearts of persecuting usurpers, that without a legal incorporation of religious and civil polity, neither could be supported." But he felt that this happy state of affairs should never be taken for granted: we should be ceaselessly vigilant against those who seek to undermine this principle of separation. "Strongly guarded as is the separation between Religion & Gov[ernmen]t in the Constitution of the United States, the danger of encroachment by Ecclesiastical Bodies, may be illustrated by precedents already furnished in their short history," he warned. He feared and deplored the "old error, that without some sort of alliance or coalition between Gov[ernmen]t & Religion neither can be duly supported. Such indeed is the tendency to such a coalition, and such its corrupting influence on both the parties, that the danger cannot be too carefully guarded ag[ain]st. . . . *Every new & successful example therefore of a perfect separation between ecclesiastical and civil matters, is of importance*" [italics mine].

Twelve years later the Reverend Jasper Adams challenged Madison's idea that Christianity had no connection with the civil government of the United States, insisting instead that "the people of the United States have retained the Christian religion as the foundation of their civil, legal, and political institutions." This claim, it is important to note, is still being made with great spirit by modern Christian politicians and organizations, who assert that the philosophical foundation of the Constitution and the Bill of Rights directly derive from biblical principles. Madison wrote a long and extremely thoughtful letter in reply, respectfully rejecting his friend's central thesis. He pointed to the example of the Southern states for emphasis:

> And if we turn to the Southern States where there was, previous to the Declaration of independence, a legal provision for the support of Religion; and since that event a surrender of it to a spontaneous support by the people, it may be said that the difference amounts nearly to a contrast in the greater purity & industry of the Pastors and in the greater devotion of their flocks, in the latter period than in the former. In Virginia the contrast is particularly striking, to those whose memories can make the comparison. . . . [T]he existing character, distinguished as it is by its religious features, and the lapse of time now more than 50 years since the legal support of Religion was withdrawn sufficiently prove that it does not need the support of Gov[ernmen]t. . . .

Madison was noticing what was becoming a peculiarly American phenomenon: namely, that full religious freedom, protected by the Constitution, seemed actually to foster religion and fan its flames rather than to spread atheism, as its opponents had feared. There could be no doubt about it: Americans, especially in the once-skeptical Southern states, were becoming more and more pious. Religious freedom had created an explosion of thriving sects, just as free-market capitalism was creating an explosion of new wealth. But this, perhaps, was not quite what Madison and Jefferson had had in mind.

CHAPTER SIX

Hamilton

🗶 ALEXANDER HAMILTON, the youngest of the six Founding Fathers discussed in this book, had as much influence as any of them upon what the new nation was to become. Perhaps more, for in the words of Henry Cabot Lodge, "We look in vain for a man who, in an equal space of time, has produced such direct and lasting effects upon our institutions and history." As the first person to urge the necessity of revising the Articles of Confederation and subsequently of creating an entire new constitution, he changed the course of American history. As the largest contributor to the *Federalist Papers* (he wrote fifty-one of the essays to Madison's twenty-nine and Jay's five) he helped formulate the intellectual foundation and justification for the American republic. As George Washington's closest associate, first as military aide-de-camp, then as political adviser, and finally as America's first secretary of the treasury, Hamilton greatly added to the great man's sheen; Washington's prestige, probity, and unerring political instincts combined with Hamilton's dazzling intellect to create a team that was unbeatable for as long as it lasted.

It was probably in the role of treasury secretary that Hamilton made his most enduring impact. His biographer, Ron Chernow, has described his achievement after five and a half years in office:

He had prevailed in almost every program he had sponsored—whether the [national] bank, assumption [of state debt by the federal government after the Revolution], funding the public debt, the tax system, the customs service, or the Coast Guard. . . . John Quincy Adams later stated that his financial system "operated like enchantment for the restoration of public credit." . . . He had laid the foundation for both liberal democracy and capitalism and helped to transform the role of the president from passive administrator to active policy maker, creating the institutional scaffolding for America's future energies as a great power.

But Hamilton was an innovator in another area too, one that is less praiseworthy and accordingly receives less press from his admirers: he pioneered, in this country, the practice of playing upon the citizenry's religious sentiments and prejudices in the interest of partisan politics. He would certainly have agreed with Seneca's dictum that "Religion is regarded by the common people as true, by the wise as foolish, and by the rulers as useful": he himself was a ruler. Hamilton's work anticipated those of the countless American political fixers who have sought to equate religiosity with morality and to associate both with their own candidates, simultaneously denigrating their rivals as atheists and libertines.

Hamilton's own religious career was erratic. Pious at certain moments of his life, he was at other times thoroughly irreligious and was never a churchgoer except during his youth. Moreover he himself was the libertine he so often accused others of being: romantically linked to his sister-in-law, he also carried on for years a sordid liaison with a woman who can only be described as a grifter.

Hamilton's early years were traumatic, even tragic: of all the Revolutionary generation's rags-to-riches stories, his is probably the most extreme. He was born in Nevis in the West Indies, the illegitimate son of an impoverished Scot and a disreputable woman who had been imprisoned for adultery. It is not even certain, in fact, whether James Hamilton was actually his father at all. During his childhood the family moved to St. Croix, where the putative father soon abandoned the family; not long afterward the mother, Rachel, died and Alexander and his brother were thenceforth shuttled between various connections and relatives. At an early age the highly intelligent Alexander was put to work as a clerk in an import-export business.

Hamilton's mother was a French Huguenot, his father a Presbyterian, and he was well versed in Calvinist practices and precepts as a child. The evangelical Great Awakening of the 1740s had reached even the provincial backwater of St. Croix, and Hamilton fell under its sway in the person of the charismatic and sympathetic Reverend Hugh Knox, the Scottish minister of Christiansted's First Presbyterian Church. Personal influence probably had a great deal to do with this, for Knox recognized and encouraged the boy's unusual talents. In any case, the fervor emanating from his pulpit rubbed off on Hamilton. The following newspaper article describing a violent storm, the teenaged Hamilton's first published work, demonstrates the influence of Knox's rhetoric:

> Where now, oh! vile worm, is all thy boasted fortitude and resolution? What is become of thine arrogance and self-sufficiency? Why dost thou tremble and stand aghast? How humble, how helpless, how contemptible you now appear. And for why? The jarring of elements—the discord of clouds? Oh! impotent presumptuous fool! . . . Death comes rushing on in triumph, veiled in a mantle of tenfold darkness. . . . And oh! thou wretch, look still a little further. See the gulf of eternal misery open. There mayest thou shortly plunge—the just reward of thy vileness. Alas! whither canst thou fly? Where hide thyself?

Hamilton's talents earned him the friendship and support of some of St. Croix's leading citizens, who now pooled their resources so that he could to go the northern colonies for a proper education. He was initially sent to Elizabethtown Academy in New Jersey, where he attracted two influential new sponsors, the political radical and early proponent of church/state separation William Livingston, and the pious philanthropist Elias Boudinot: these two men would soon become New Jersey's leaders in the Revolutionary struggle. In Elizabethtown, Hamilton regularly attended the town's Presbyterian meetinghouse, but he also came under the influence of Thomas Bradbury Chandler, the Anglican minister of the nearby Church of St. John, a future Loyalist who advocated the appointment of bishops to America for the purpose of suppressing the non-Episcopal sects like the Presbyterians.

Hamilton planned to attend Princeton, which he preferred to the Anglican King's College (later Columbia University) in New York because under the direction of John Witherspoon it was definitely, as one of his friends said, "more *republican*." His sponsors in St. Croix, too, favored this choice. But in the end Witherspoon rejected Hamilton's request to accelerate his course of studies, so Hamilton repaired to King's. There, it seems, he himself became an Anglican, and a pious one at that. Churchgoing was a rigorous affair at King's, with prayers said several times a day and two church services on Sundays. Hamilton's roommate, Robert Troup, described his friend's devotional routine:

> Whilst at college, [he] was attentive to public worship, and in the habit of praying upon his knees both night and morning. I have lived in the same room with him for sometime and I have often been powerfully affected by the fervor and eloquence of his prayers. [He] had [already] read most of the polemical writers on religious subjects and he was a zealous believer in the fundamental doctrines of Christianity.

Hamilton was soon caught up in the Revolutionary movement. King's, a bastion of Anglicanism, was a Loyalist stronghold. Hamilton took the Revolutionary side, quickly becoming one of the cause's most rousing and valuable pamphleteers. His first effort, *A Full Vindication*, was published in 1774, and more soon followed, including a fourteen-essay series on the political crisis called *The Monitor*, published in the *New-York Journal* in 1775–1776.

Hamilton's formal education was interrupted by the war. He joined the Continental Army while still a student and led a daring nighttime attack of one hundred men against the lighthouse at Sandy Hook. When Hamilton crossed to New Jersey with General Washington after the Battle of Harlem Heights, his talents soon came to the leader's attention and he became his aide-de-camp, eventually serving through most of the war as what amounted to Washington's chief of staff, in which capacity his fluent French, learned from his Huguenot mother, made him invaluable as a diplomatic link with Lafayette and the other French officers.

After the war Hamilton finished his legal studies and quickly became the preeminent lawyer in New York. In 1784 he drafted the constitution for the Bank of New York and became its director and attorney. His involvement in politics continued, and so far as the mixture of politics with religion went he seems to have adopted a Madisonian, separationist stance. He himself, with maturity, had apparently become too busy for his former pious practices, and for many years had almost nothing to do with religion unless it could be seen to have some political use. His "Second Letter from Phocion" of 1784 states his philosophy: there is really not much to choose between it and that of his eventual nemesis, Jefferson.

> There is a bigotry in politics, as well as in religions, equally pernicious in both. The zealots, of either description, are ignorant of the advantage of a spirit of toleration: It was a long time before the kingdoms of Europe were convinced of the folly of persecutions, with respect to those, who were schismatics from the established church. The cry was, these

people will be equally the disturbers of the hierarchy and of the state. While some states were impoverishing and depopulating themselves, by their severities to the non-conformists, their wiser neighbors were reaping the fruits of their folly, and augmenting their own numbers, industry and wealth, by receiving with open arms the persecuted fugitives. Time and experience have taught a different lesson; and there is not an enlightened nation, which does not now acknowledge the force of this truth, that whatever speculative notions of religion may be entertained, men will not on that account, be enemies to a government, that affords them protection and security.

This excerpt contains some standard phrases common to much of liberal Enlightenment rhetoric. "Zeal" is used in a negative sense (as it would not be, in political circles, today); "enlightened" in a positive way, one that implies religious skepticism; religion itself is seen in terms of "speculative notions," a formulation of pure skepticism. Toleration, or better yet, "what is far more precious than mere religious toleration—a perfect equality of religious privileges," is seen not only as a humane principle but as a path to national wealth. Voltaire's observations about London's Royal Exchange had provided the classic template for this idea: "There the Jew, the Mahometan, and the Christian transact together as though they all professed the same religion, and give the name of Infidel to none but bankrupts. . . . If one religion only were allowed in England, the government would very possibly become arbitrary; if there were but two, the people would cut one another's throats; but as there are such a multitude, they all live happy and in peace."

Hamilton's thinking, unlike that of his philosophical colleagues (and enemies) Jefferson and Adams, was always directed toward practical goals: his brain was focused on action and power rather than on thought for its own sake. Thus when he made a reflection

such as the following, it was because he planned to direct his conclusions into politically or financially advantageous channels:

> The supposition of universal venality in human nature is little
> less an error in political reasoning than the supposition of
> universal rectitude. The institution of delegated power implies
> that there is a portion of virtue and honor among mankind,
> which may be a reasonable foundation of confidence. And
> experience justifies the theory.

This musing draws all its logic from the empirical spirit of Enlightenment skepticism rather than from the system of Christian
ethics with which Hamilton grew up and from which his political career was drawing him ever farther. After the Revolution he attended
the Confederation Congress as one of New York State's five delegates and quickly became its leading light, along with James Madison. These two most brilliant men of the Revolution's younger generation were also the most vocal and persuasive in the cause of
jettisoning the old Articles of Confederation and creating a proper
constitution possessed of strong centralized powers. Hamilton defended the principles of the new Constitution, including the "no establishment" clause, with consummate lawyerly skill in the *Federalist
Papers*. When some objected to the office of the presidency, saying
that a president would too closely resemble a king, Hamilton objected loudly, stressing the purely secular nature of the proposed office: ". . . The one has no particle of spiritual juristdiction: The other
is the supreme head and Governor of the national church! What answer shall we give to those who would persuade us that things so unlike resemble each other?"

The Constitution itself, as disgruntled Christians have frequently
pointed out, contains no mention whatever of God. Hamilton was on
the committee of Style and Arrangement for the Constitution (along
with, among others, the non-Christian Gouverneur Morris), and
while God's presence was not necessary to the Constitution—it

would have worked against the document's determinedly secular tone—Hamilton deemed that it *was* necessary to Washington's 1797 Farewell Address, which Hamilton drafted before the first president's retirement. These phrases, which have become indelibly associated with Washington (who personally paid little attention to the Christian religion), are actually the work of Hamilton, who had already learned the lesson that public expressions of piety cannot be dispensed with by those who wish to control the masses.

> Cherish good faith and Justice towards, and peace and harmony with all nations. Religion and morality enjoin this conduct. And It cannot be, but that true policy equally demands it. It will be worthy of a free enlightened and at no distant period a great nation to give to mankind the magnanimous and too novel example of a people invariably governed by those exalted views. Who can doubt that in a long course of time and events the fruits of such a conduct would richly repay any temporary advantages which might be lost by a steady adherence to the plan? Can it be that Providence has not connected the permanent felicity of a nation with its virtue?
> . . . Nor ought we to flatter ourselves that morality can be separated from religion. Concede as much as may be asked to the effect of refined education in minds of a peculiar structure—can we believe—can we in prudence suppose that national morality can be maintained in exclusion of religious principles? Does it not require the aid of a generally received and divinely authoritative Religion?

There is a certain irony in the fact that these words were written by a man not known for his strict ahderence to morality, to say the least, to be put into the mouth of a man who, though himself of the highest personal morality, was not particularly pious. But this type of easy hypocrisy has become so commonplace in American politics since that time that it is hard to take it seriously.

During the Adams administration Hamilton exerted an enormous amount of energy in trying to control the government from behind the scenes through his cronies from the Washington cabinet
whom Adams had unwisely kept on in his. Neither Adams nor
Washington was much inclined to use religion for political purposes;
Hamilton, on the other hand, saw it as a great mine of untapped opportunity. He himself strongly believed that Adams ought to take
advantage of American religiosity as a way of drumming up popular
support for what then seemed an inevitable war against revolutionary France. Here, in a letter to William Loughton Smith, he explains
his ideas in remarkably Machiavellian terms:

> In addition to these [military] measures it may be proper by
> some religious solemnity to impress seriously the minds of the
> People. A philosopher may regard the present course of things
> in Europe as some great providential dispensation. A Christian
> can hardly view it in any other light. Both these descriptions of
> persons must approve a national appeal to Heaven for
> protection. The politician will consider this as an important
> means of influencing Opinion, and will think it a valuable
> resource in a contest with France to set the Religious Ideas of
> his Countrymen in active Competition with the Atheistical
> tenets of their enemies. This is an advantage which we shall be
> very unskilful, if we do not improve to the utmost. And the
> impulse cannot be too early given. I am persuaded a day of
> humiliation and prayer besides being very proper would be
> extremely useful.

This wonderful letter should be better known—indeed, it
should be canonized as one of the classic texts of the founding of the
United States, for it sets out with remarkable neatness and honesty
one of the great ruling principles of the republic: the practice of
Bible-thumping as "an important means of influencing Opinion";
the rallying of jingoism and militarism through the setting of "the

Religious Ideas of [the politician's] Countrymen in active Competition with the Atheistical [or fanatical, nowadays] tenets of their enemies." What makes Hamilton's comments so striking is his straightforward admission of opportunism.

Hamilton passed these thoughts on to his friend James McHenry, secretary of war in Adams's cabinet.

> . . . [L]et the President recommend a day to be observed as a day of fasting humiliation & prayer. On religious ground this is very proper—On political, it is very expedient. The Government will be very unwise if it does not make the most of the religious preposessions of our people—opposing the honest enthusiasm of Religious Opinion to the phrenzy of Political fanaticism.

And in another letter:

> In such a crisis this appears to me proper in itself, and it will be politically useful to impress our nation that there is a serious state of things—to strengthen religious ideas in a contest, which in its progress may require that our people may consider themselves as the defenders of their country against atheism, conquest, and anarchy.

This is a policy Hamilton's political heirs have practiced to great effect, right down to George W. Bush and his War on Terror. Adams in the end was persuaded by the logic and proclaimed a day of "solemn humiliation, fasting and prayer" for May 9, 1798. It was a decision Adams was doubtful about at the time and came bitterly to regret later on, even blaming it for his defeat in the 1800 election.

During the months leading up to that election, Hamilton did his very best to undermine the nascent Republican party and its most powerful figure, Jefferson. He even secretly proposed to John Jay that they meddle with the electoral process in New York to that end: "In times like these in which we live, it will not do to be overscrupulous.

It is easy to sacrifice the substantial interests of a society by a strict adherence to ordinary rules." Such rules "ought not to hinder the taking
of a *legal* and *constitutional* step, to prevent an *Atheist* in Religion and a
Fanatic in politics from getting possession of the helm of the State."
(This philosophy has been shared by Richard Nixon and George W.
Bush, among other recent American statesmen.) One of the principal
ways Hamilton tried to achieve his end was to launch a smear campaign against the Virginian, portraying him whenever possible as a
godless and amoral man who would degrade the tone of the office and
let the country lapse into degeneracy. He defeated his own purpose,
however, by failing to control his personal animus against the leading
Federalist candidate, Adams, writing a truly scurrilous pamphlet
against him which did great damage both to Adams himself and to
Hamilton's own Federalist party.

In any case the people, at least at that time, turned out not to be
quite as malleable as Hamilton had hoped, and there was considerable backlash against his smears. One of the most eloquent opponents of Hamiltonian rhetoric was the anti-clerical activist Abraham
Bishop, who in his 1800 address to the Phi Beta Kappa Society at
Yale asked the students to use their discernment and common sense
regarding the political scene. "How much, think you," he asked,
"has religion benefited by sermons, intended to show that Satan and
Cain were jacobins? How much by sermons in which every deistical
argument has been presented with its greatest force as being a part
of the republican creed? . . . The people, instead of being alarmed
lest religion should suffer under a new administration, ought to be
infinitely solicitous to wrest the protection of it from those who are
using it as a state engine"—a warning that still holds good today.
Later, after Jefferson's election, Bishop returned to the subject in another oration. "[When] the pretended friends of religion lead infidel lives; when they carry religion to market and offer it in exchange
for luxuries and honors; when they place it familiarly and constantly
in the columns of newspapers, *manifestly connected with electioneering*

purposes, and when they are offering it up as a morning and evening sacrifice on the altar of political party—these men are placing a firebrand to every meeting house and applying a torch to every bible."

The attack on Jefferson's irreligion was in fact to backfire badly; the general population turned out to be a little more sophisticated than Hamilton had given them credit for. Most informed voters knew perfectly well that a Jefferson administration was no more likely than any other to sink the nation into moral depravity. When to everyone's surprise Aaron Burr tied with Jefferson in the first ballot, leaving Adams out of the running in third place, Hamilton felt considerable discomfiture, for Burr really *was* the libertine Hamilton had accused Jefferson of being—"truly the *Catiline* of America," as he said. Now Hamilton was forced not only to lend his support to the hated Jefferson, but honestly to assess the personal qualities of this longtime foe for the first time. Jefferson, he now grudgingly admitted, was "By far not so dangerous a man [as Burr] and he has pretensions to character."

The Federalist party, which had been largely Hamilton's creation, was effectively dead. It never won another presidential election, and Hamilton himself would not hold political office again. Nevertheless he continued to work his influence behind the scenes. One of his most interesting schemes, from the perspective of our twenty-first century alliance between Christian organizations and conservative politics, was the proposed creation of a "Christian Constitutional Society." In a letter to Federalist congressman James A. Bayard he outlined this plan, stressing above all its political utility.

> Nothing is more fallacious than to expect to produce any valuable or permanent results, in political projects, by relying merely on the reason of men. Men are rather reasoning than reasonable animals and for the most part governed by the impulse of passion. This is a truth well understood by our adversaries [the Republicans] who have practised upon it with

no small benefit to their cause. For at the very moment they are
eulogizing the reason of men & professing to appeal only to
that faculty, they are courting the strongest & most active
passion of the human heart—VANITY!

    ... I now offer you the outline of the plan. ... Let an
Association be formed to be denominated, "The Christian
Constitutional Society." It's objects to be

    1st The support of the Christian Religion.

    2nd The support of the Constitution of the United States.

Its Organization.

    1st A directing council consisting of a President & 12
Members, of whom 4 & the President to be a quorum.

    2nd A sub-directing council in each State consisting of a
Vice-President & 12 members, of whom 4 with the Vice-
President to be a quorum & 3rd As many societies in each
State, as local circumstances may permit to be formed by the
Sub-directing council.

The Meeting at Washington to Nominate the *President* & *Vice-
President* together with *4 Members of each* of the councils, who
are to complete their own numbers respectively.

Its Means.

    1st The diffusion of information. For this purpose not
only the Newspapers but pamphlets must be largely employed
& to do this a fund must be created. 5 dollars annually for 8
years, to be contributed by each member who can really
afford it, (taking care not to burden the less able brethren)
may afford a competent fund for a competent time. It is
essential to be able to disseminate *gratis* useful publications.
Whenever it can be done, & there is a press, clubs should be
formed to meet once a week, read the newspapers & prepare
essays paragraphs &ct.

2nd The use of all lawful means in concert to promote the election of *fit men*. A lively correspondence must be kept up between the different Societies.

3rd The promoting of institutions of a charitable & useful nature in the management of the Foederalists. The populous cities ought particularly to be attended to. Perhaps it will be well to institute in such places 1st Societies for the relief of Emigrants—2nd. Academies each with one professor for instructing the different Classes of Mechanics in the principles of Mechanics & Elements of Chemistry. . . .

Hamilton's piety had been for many years merely opportunistic, but with the 1801 dueling death of his eldest son, Philip, he sought true comfort in religion and became, perhaps for the first time since early youth, a sincere Christian. His own death in 1804 was eerily reminiscent of his son's, and the last two centuries have seen a great deal of speculation as to why Hamilton did not pull the trigger during his fateful duel with Aaron Burr. Was he depressed? Was this a form of suicide? But Hamilton's own explanation was simple and credible, and there is no reason not to take it seriously:

> The Scruples of a Christian [he wrote to his wife before the duel] have determined me to expose my own life to any extent rather than subject my self to the guilt of taking the life of another. This must increase my hazards & redoubles my pangs for you. But you had rather I should die innocent than live guilty. Heaven can preserve me and I humbly hope will but in the contrary event, I charge you to remember that you are a Christian. God's will be done. The will of a merciful God must be good.

Unlike the supposedly devout Washington, the renegade Hamilton wished desperately to have a minister present at his deathbed, and when it became clear that he was mortally wounded

he asked for one. But now Hamilton's illegitimate birth and skeptical past came back to haunt him: New York's men of God, in their
wisdom, were not eager to help this by now truly penitent soul to
meet its Maker. Although in the months before his death Hamilton
had conducted family prayers at home, he had not attended a church
since his college days. Now Benjamin Moore, New York's Episcopal bishop, refused to give the dying Hamilton communion on the
grounds that he had not been baptized and was not a regular churchgoer. Hamilton then sent for a Presbyterian pastor, who informed
him that he could receive communion only in church. Moore was
summoned once again, and finally served communion to the dying
man, but only grudgingly and after delivering a stern lecture on the
sinfulness of dueling.

So while Hamilton "got" religion shortly before his death, this
newly won faith had no effect on the enormous contributions he had
made to the new nation. During his youth he heartily supported his
Virginian colleagues in their efforts to keep God out of the Constitution, to forbid religious establishments, and to promote full religious liberty; later, when he did try to introduce piety into the public discourse, it was for the base purpose of electioneering rather than
as a sincere ideological effort to break down the wall of separation. If
the heroes of the five preceding chapters appear from our perspective as rather idealized Enlightenment philosopher-kings, the practical and hard-nosed Hamilton points the way toward the future, and
to our own era of violent political partisanship and religious huck-
sterism.

CHAPTER SEVEN

1787 and Beyond

When the war was over and the victory over our
enemies won, and the blessings and happiness of
liberty and peace were secured, the Constitution was
framed and God was neglected. He was not merely
forgotten. He was absolutely voted out of the
Constitution. The proceedings, as published by
Thompson, the secretary, and the history of the day,
show that the question was gravely debated whether
God should be in the Constitution or not, and, after a
solemn debate he was deliberately voted out of it. . . .
There is not only in the theory of our government no
recognition of God's laws and sovereignty, but its
practical operation, its administration, has been
conformable to its theory. Those who have been called
to administer the government have not been men
making any public profession of Christianity. . . .

—Reverend Bird Wilson, sermon on the "Religion of
the Presidents," *Albany Daily Advertiser,* 1831

☙ THESE SENTIMENTS, vented by the same Dr. Bird Wilson who researched George Washington's religious beliefs, formulate the feelings of many American Christians who are distressed over what they see as the absence of God in our Constitution. Such people have often chosen to justify the all-too-evident godlessness of the document by claiming that its framers were so godly, so thoroughly steeped in Christianity, that God was implicit in everything they did. There was no need for the founders to write about God and Christianity in the Constitution since it was understood by all that a Christian God and a Christian agenda were an integral part of the project.

But any perusal of the proceedings of the Constitutional Convention, as Dr. Wilson discovered, shows that this was definitely not the case. The framers, as a group, saw religion as a divisive rather than a cohesive force and appear to have decided that the less said about it the better, so long as the concept of full religious freedom was made clear and enforceable. Thus while the 1781 Articles of Confederation had acknowledged "the Great Governor of the World," the Constitution acknowledged no supernatural authority at all, not even that vaguest of deist formulations, "Providence."

Of the thirteen states represented at the Constitutional Convention, all had established religions written into their state constitutions except for Virginia and New York. The framers of the Constitution basically followed the example of these two states, especially Virginia's with its legally binding Statute for Religious Freedom.

There was surprisingly little debate or controversy over this decision at the time. The inequality and social unrest caused by the British Test Acts, which had curtailed the political and civil rights of so many British subjects, were only too apparent when viewed from this side of the Atlantic, and a "no religious test" clause was favored by many of the delegates, including some of the most fervent Christians in the group. It was formally proposed on August 20, 1787, by Charles Pinckney of South Carolina; there were a few minor objections, mostly on the grounds that such a clause was unnecessary given, in the words of Roger Sherman, the prevailing "liberality." It was passed, according to the Maryland delegate Luther Martin, "by a very great majority of the convention, and without much debate." In fact, so far as we know, no delegate at the convention endorsed any positive role at all for religion in the government.

The pertinent part of Article 6, Section 3, of the Constitutition, then, reads as follows: federal officials "shall be bound by Oath or Affirmation, to support this Constitution; but no religious Test shall ever be required as a Qualification to any Office or public Trust under the United States." As Madison wrote with satisfaction, "The door of the Federal Government, is open to merit of every description, whether native or adoptive, whether young or old, and without regard to poverty or wealth, or to any particular profession of religious faith."

Of course that is exactly what scared a lot of people. A delegate at the Massachusetts ratifying convention, for one, worried that if the president were not required to take a religious oath of formal adherence to the Protestant faith, "a Turk, a Jew, a Roman Catholic, and what is worse than all, a Universalist [Unitarian] may be President of the United States." Such fears were pooh-poohed by the more rational, however. Governor Samuel Johnston of North Carolina voiced the commonsense approach:

> When I heard there were apprehensions that the pope of Rome could be the President of the United States, I was greatly astonished. It might as well be said that the king of England, or France, or the Grand Turk, could be chosen to that office. It would have been as good an argument. It appears to me that it would have been dangerous if Congress could intermeddle with the subject of religion. True religion is derived from a much higher source than human laws.

In the event, the defenders of the "no religious test" clause carried the day rather easily. This was partly due to its broad support from the rapidly growing numbers of Baptists, Methodists, and members of other sects who had long chafed in their subordinate role as "dissenters." These people had no wish to continue as second-class citizens in a nation controlled by Anglicans or Presbyterians.

Isaac Backus, an influential Baptist minister who served as a delegate to the Massachusetts ratifying convention, was a passionate advocate of the "no religious test" clause and proved a powerful ally of Madison and Hamilton in its defense. As he said:

> Many appear to be much concerned about it; but nothing is more evident, both in reason and the Holy Scriptures, than that religion is ever a matter between God and individuals; and, therefore, no man or men can impose any *religious test*, without invading the essential prerogatives of our God Jesus Christ. Ministers first assumed this power under the Christian name; and then Constantine approved of the practice, when he adopted the profession of Christianity, as an engine of state policy. And let the history of all nations be searched from that day to this, and it will appear that the imposing of *religious tests* hath been the greatest engine of tyranny in the world. And I rejoice to see so many gentlemen, who are now giving in their rights of conscience in this great and important matter. Some serious minds discover a concern lest, if all *religious tests* should be excluded, the Congress would hereafter establish Popery, or some other tyrannical way of worship. But it is most certain that no such way of worship can be established without any *religious test*.

The clause had countless other clerical supporters, not only dissenting ones but Anglicans and Presbyterians as well.

At the Constitutional Convention Madison actually proposed two clauses that were rejected by the assembly. They were, first, that

> The civil rights of none shall be abridged on account of religious belief or worship, nor shall any national religion be

established, nor shall the full and equal rights of conscience be in any manner, or on any pretext infringed.

And, that

No state shall violate the equal rights of conscience, or the freedom of the press, or the trial by jury in criminal cases.

Had these measures passed, religious regulation would have been forbidden on the state level as well as the federal. As it stood, however, when the Constitution and the Bill of Rights were passed, including the First Amendment prohibiting the establishment of a national religion, most of the state constitutions still did not conform with these principles. The constitutions of eleven of the thirteen states—that is, every state excluding New York and Virginia—retained established sects and religious tests. Madison, the greatest and most stubborn advocate of religious liberty among the Constitution's framers, enjoined the states to follow the example of the federal government and to "hasten to revise & purify your systems, and make the example of your Country as pure & compleat, in what relates to the freedom of the mind and its allegiance to its maker, as in what belongs to the legitimate objects of political & civil institutions."

This eventually happened, but not nearly as quickly as Madison, Hamilton, and the other proponents of religious freedom would have liked. Pennsylvania dropped its religious test laws in 1790, Delaware in 1792, Georgia and South Carolina soon afterward, but Vermont and New Jersey retained tests until 1844. Disestablishment on the state level proceeded slowly, especially in the Presbyterian and Congregational strongholds of New England: the Congregational church was disestablished in New Hampshire in 1817, in Connecticut a year later, in Maine in 1820, and at long last in Massachusetts in 1833. The Fourteenth Amendment of 1868, enacted in the wake of the tragically destructive Civil War, ruled that "No State shall make or enforce any law which shall abridge the privileges or immunities of citizens of the United States; nor shall any State deprive any person of life, liberty, or property, without due process of law." State laws were thus legally superseded by federal ones; still, New Hampshire did not end religious tests until 1877, nor Maryland, amazingly enough, until 1961, when a Supreme Court ruling finally put an end to this relic of the bad old days.

The 1797 Treaty of Tripoli illustrates the triumph, temporarily at least, of Madisonian separationism. In that year the federal government concluded a "Treaty of Peace and Friendship between the United States of America and the Bey and Subjects of Tripoli, or Barbary," now known simply as the Treaty of Tripoli. Article 11 of the treaty contains these words:

> As the Government of the United States . . . *is not in any sense founded on the Christian religion* [italics mine]—as it has in itself no character of enmity against the laws, religion, or tranquillity of Musselmen—and as the said States never had entered into any war or act of hostility against any Mehomitan nation, it is declared by the parties that no pretext arising from religious opinions shall ever produce an interruption of the harmony existing between the two countries.

This document was endorsed by President John Adams and Secretary of State Timothy Pickering. It was then sent to the Senate for ratification; the vote was unanimous. It is worth pointing out that although this was the 339th time a recorded vote had been required by the Senate, it was only the third unanimous vote in the Senate's history. There is no record of debate or dissent. The text of the treaty was printed in full in the *Philadelphia Gazette* and in two New York papers, but there were no screams·of outrage, as one might expect today.

But there were plenty who resisted the full religious implications of the Constitution. During the Washington and Adams administrations, Christian lawmakers at the federal level lobbied for, and achieved, tax exemptions for church property, chaplains for Congress and the armed services, and presidential decrees for days of thanksgiving. As we have seen, James Madison's notes and letters show that he, the chief architect of the Constitution, believed these concessions to be unconstitutional. But the times were definitely changing.

The Second Great Awakening, which began at the close of the eighteenth century and had such a very surprising effect on the election of 1800, would change the climate of the country for at least the next century; in many ways its attitudes are still with us. A new religiosity swept the nation, bringing the American Enlightenment to an abrupt end. The excesses of the French Revolution, the conservative reaction in Europe and America, and the growing influence of evangelical sects quickly pushed the skeptical eighteenth century into obsolescence. In 1800 the Federalist power brokers saw Jefferson's godlessness as his greatest political vulnerability. They turned out to be wrong, but by then the idea of religious slander as a political weapon had taken root, and it is still with us today.

The War of 1812 persuaded many pious Americans that it had been a big mistake to leave God out of the government. Timothy Dwight, the president of Yale, expressed this opinion to his students:

> The nation has offended Providence. We formed our
> Constitution without any acknowledgement of God; without
> any recognition of His mercies to us, as a people, of His
> government, or even of His existence. The [Constitutional]
> Convention, by which it was formed, never asked even once,
> His direction, or His blessings, upon their labours. Thus we
> commenced our national existence, under the present system,
> without God.

America turned to religious fundamentalism, and a great many, then as now, saw this as a blessing. Virginia's John Randolph for instance, cousin of the revolutionary Edmund Randolph, wrote in 1815 that

> A change has certainly been wrought in Virginia, the most ungodly country on the face of the earth, where the Gospel has ever been preached. I flatter myself that it is the case elsewhere in the U.S. . . . The last was a generation of free thinkers, disciples of Hume & Voltaire & Bolingbroke, & there are very few persons, my dear Rutledge, of our years who have not received their first impressions from the same die. . . . there are however some striking instances in this country, as well as in Europe, of men of the first abilities devoting themselves to the service of the only true God.

A quarter of the way through the century—at the symbolic moment of Jefferson's and Adams's deaths—the transformation seemed complete. By 1832 Mrs. Frances Trollope, visiting from England, commented on the depressing fact that "Rousseau, Voltaire, Diderot, &c, were read by the old federalists, but now they seem known more as naughty words, than as great names." While in 1776 only 17 percent of Americans had officially belonged to a church, that figure had doubled by 1832.

During the Civil War, those who had always resented the godless Constitution attempted to amend the document to recognize Jesus Christ as the source of American authority and law. A group of these men, calling themselves the National Reform Association, proposed to reword the Preamble thus:

> We, the people of the United States, humbly acknowledging Almighty God as the source of all authority and power in civil government, The Lord Jesus Christ as the Governor among the Nations, and His revealed will as of supreme authority, in order to constitute a Christian government . . . do ordain and establish this Constitution for the United States of America.

One can only imagine the reaction of Gouverneur Morris, the freethinking sophisticate who authored the original Preamble. Luckily this project came to nothing: when the Association urged Abraham Lincoln to adopt this new Preamble he was courteous but noncommittal (in the tradition of George Washington), and nothing was done about it. So far, the Preamble stands as it was originally written.

Interpretation of the Constitution's religious clauses—Article 6, clause 3, and the First Amendment—are still being tussled over by the Supreme Court, and probably always will be. Justice Hugo Black's 1947 decision in *Everson v. Board of Education* would seem to have been pretty straightforward:

> The "establishment of religion" clause of the First Amendment means at least this: Neither a state nor the Federal Government can set up a church. Neither can pass laws which aid one religion, aid all religions, or prefer one religion over another. Neither can force nor influence a person to go to or to remain away from church against his will or force him to profess a belief or disbelief in any religion. No person can be punished for entertaining or professing religious beliefs or disbeliefs, for church attendance or non-attendance. No tax in any amount, large or small, can be levied to support any religious activities or institutions, whatever they may be called, or whatever form they may adopt to teach or practice religion. Neither a state nor the Federal Government can, openly or secretly, participate in the affairs of any religious organizations or groups and vice versa. In the words of Jefferson, the clause against establishment of religion by law was intended to erect "a wall of separation between Church and State."

But this decision and others have not stopped Christian anti-separationists from asserting, tirelessly and incorrectly, that Jefferson did not mean by the words "wall of separation" what we mean; that our Founding Fathers were good Christians; and that modern "secularism" does not correspond with the founders' ideas. Some religious groups even claim that the Constitution was designed on Christian principles and with the purpose of perpetuating Christianity, and a surprising number of people have accepted this statement without a significant challenge.

Many have remarked upon the irony that this country of no established religion has produced a far more religiously zealous populace than most countries *with* established Christian churches: the contrast is particularly striking with the mother country, England, in which church membership has long been on the wane. Americans have even retained, though informally, the religious tests the Founding Fathers deleted from the federal government. As Isaac Kramnick and R. Laurence Moore noted in *Our Godless Constitution*, "To declare oneself a nontheist is de facto to disqualify oneself for the office of the president of the United States. One's religion is more of an issue in this country of religious disestablishment than in most countries where religious establishment still exists. . . . This country, which abandoned an established church first, has kept an informal test for its highest office the longest." This is absolutely true, and it is a very brave politician, or maybe a foolhardy one, who admits to being anything less than a devout, churchgoing Christian. Far from having to fear that "the pope of Rome" or "the Great Turk" will win the presidency, it seems that we are not even ready, more than two hundred years after the easy ratification of the "no religious test" clause, to elect a Jew or an agnostic to that office.

For most of our history the religious pretensions of our chief executives have stayed within certain boundaries, tacitly understood since the days of George Washington. Both conventionally pious presidents and freethinking ones treated their religion as their own business and made no attempt to impose their standards on society. The American population returned the favor, and religious fundamentalists were for the most part content to practice their faith in freedom without trying to have their theological tenets written into the law of the land. This continued to be true beyond the Revolutionary Era and even into our own. Franklin Roosevelt was able to lead the nation in prayer on D-day without giving the impression that he was forcing a Christian agenda on the populace. Jimmy Carter, a self-described evangelical Christian, observed a strict respect for the spirit as well as the letter of church/state separation, and made no claims that his personal beliefs should be representative of the general population. And all modern presidents have invoked the deity (though not Jesus Christ) in their inaugural addresses, without anything particular being made of it.

It was only in the 1980s that the lines began seriously to blur. Ronald Reagan's proclamation of 1983 as "The Year of the Bible" would have made Madison turn in his grave; but he got away with it, incurring only minor cavils from the liberal opposition. Meanwhile the political organization of fundamentalist and evangelical Christians into a vast Republican voting bloc continued apace. The public display of religious zeal has become such a commonplace in public life that nowadays, when Bible study sessions are held in the White House and the Justice Department for staff members—a form of potential religious harassment that should be considered as unacceptable as the sexual variety—no one has the nerve to offer serious, principled opposition.

Tom Wolfe wrote recently that ours is the era of the "fifth freedom," freedom from religion, and implied that this was not exactly what our nation's founders had anticipated or hoped for. But a perusal of the founders' writings, both public and private, shows that it *was* what they worked for. Madison and Jefferson, in particular, fervently believed that freedom of religious choice included the freedom to choose no religion at all, and the Constitution was consciously designed to offer that fifth freedom to those who wish to exercise it.

CHAPTER EIGHT

The World That Produced the Founders

🏃 IT IS EASY to appreciate that each of the six Founding Fathers discussed in this book was an extraordinary personality in his own right. But the modern reader, lacking a sufficient historical education, too often sees them within a cultural vacuum and therefore fails to understand much of their political agenda. We have come to take for granted a society in which church and state are legally separated, and therefore we find it hard to comprehend just why these men felt so passionately about the issue, and what they meant (as opposed to what *we* mean) when they spoke of a secular state, or of religious freedom as compared with mere toleration. For this we must try to think and imagine ourselves back into the eighteenth-century worldview—a historical and philosophical outlook that is extremely dissimilar to our own. We live in an America that is very different, both materially and intellectually, from the one the Founding Fathers were familiar with, and if as a nation we feel that the founders and their ideas continue to have significance for our national project—and most of our leaders do claim to feel this—we should at least attempt a real understanding of what these ideas were.

We don't learn much history in school, but one idea most of us seem to have picked up is that the original colonists came to this country to escape religious persecution and to create a society with religious freedom for all.

Like most such historical simplifications, this is only partially true. Yes, some colonists were fleeing religious persecution, but just as many came here for commercial reasons, to establish plantations and trading communities chartered by the mother country, England. Virginia, the largest and financially most important English colony and the first (1607) to be settled, was originally incorporated in the manner of the British East India Company. Its purpose was to make money both for the colonists and for the merchants back in London. North and South Carolina were set up along similar lines. Georgia was originally founded as a penal colony in which to siphon off the excess, undesirable population of England.

Those who really *were* fleeing religious persecution did not by any means have in mind what we now do when we speak of religious freedom. The nineteenth-century humorist Artemus Ward got it about right with his dry assessment of the Pilgrim Fathers and their motivations: "The Puritans nobly fled from a land of despotism," he wrote, "to a land of freedom, where they could not only enjoy their own religion, but could prevent everybody else from enjoying his." The New England Congregationalists who set up the Massachussetts Bay Colony (1629) and other communities had no intention of building a society in which religious freedom could flourish: they wanted, instead, to establish a theocracy, a "City upon a Hill." As their descendant Cotton Mather later wrote, Massachusetts was "the spot of *earth*, which the God of heaven *spied* out for the seat of such *evangelical,* and *ecclesiastical*, and very remarkable transactions." The residents of the Massachusetts Bay Colony believed they had a covenant with God. All those who were outside this covenant—Anglicans, Quakers, Catholics, Baptists, not to mention Jews—were unwelcome in the community and vigorously persecuted if they had the temerity to try to settle there. Anglicans returned the compliment: Puritans who moved to Virginia were seen as a threat to the colony's peace, and were harrassed accordingly.

For an understanding of the religious diversity and passions in the thirteen American colonies and the religious settlement that would eventually be reached by the Founding Fathers, it is necessary to look back at what was going on in England as the colonists were leaving the country. England herself had been undergoing religious turmoil ever since Henry VIII had broken with the pope in 1534, severed the English church from Rome, and dissolved the monasteries. The country returned briefly to the Catholic fold during the reign of his daughter, Mary I, but the social turmoil that resulted from these changes was intense, and England risked an all-out religious war like those that were devastating the Continent. Mary's sister Elizabeth I finally came up with a working plan, called by historians "the Elizabethan settlement," whereby the Protestant Church of England, closely related in ritual to Catholicism, was established as the nation's official sect. In 1559 Elizabeth imposed the Act of Uniformity, requiring her subjects to publicly support the church. Many Catholics and dissenters whose consciences did not allow them to accept the Church of England left for the American colonies during the next century.

Those who stayed on did not have an easy life. King James I openly expressed his distaste for "papists and Puritans," lumping them together as disturbers of the peace, and he passed laws prohibiting Puritans from pronouncing public bans on activities such as Sunday sports and dances. The Puritans disapproved of him and disapproved even more of his son Charles I, whom they suspected (wrongly) of being a secret Catholic. Charles was in fact committed to the established church and strengthened the laws against dissenters. It was during his reign that the Massachussetts Bay Colony was founded.

The English Civil Wars (1642–1651) and the Commonwealth and Protectorate (1651–1660) pitted Puritan parliamentarians and

Anglican royalists against one another and further affected events on the American continent. The tensions that had long simmered between Charles I and the English Parliament broke out into full-scale war in 1642; seven years later Charles was executed, with Parliament and its Puritan general, Oliver Cromwell, assuming control of the country. The Puritans in power proved to be even more intolerant than the Stuart monarchs had been: now Anglicans and loyalists were persecuted as Puritans and other dissenters once were, and many of these came to America, settling in states with Anglican majorities like Virginia and New York. The power vacuum that followed the death of Cromwell showed that parliamentary rule was still tenuous and problematic, however, and in 1660 Charles's son Charles II was restored to the throne.

Charles II was an easygoing monarch who had no particular wish to persecute dissenters, but some kind of firm religious settlement seemed to be needed. The Clarendon Code, named for Charles's chancellor, was passed between 1661 and 1665. The idea behind this code was to bar non-Anglicans from the universities, from voting, and from holding political office. The Test Act of 1673 excluded from public office all those who refused to swear oaths of allegiance and supremacy, or who would not receive communion according to the rites of the Church of England, or who professed a belief in transubstantiation according to Roman Catholic doctrine.

It was not until the Glorious Revolution of 1688, in which Charles's intolerant brother James II was ousted in favor of his daughter, Mary, and her husband William of Orange, that dissenters from the Church of England gained significant rights. William and Mary ascended the throne through a deal by which the English monarchy would become a constitutional one ruling through and by consent of Parliament. The ancient principle of rule by divine right came permanently to an end. The new monarchs agreed, in effect, to govern with the consent of the governed.

One of the results of this constitutional monarchy was that religious dissidents gained a new measure of toleration. The Church of England was still the established one, but the 1689 Act of Toleration (passed in the same year that Locke's first *Letter Concerning Toleration* appeared) permitted non-Anglicans to worship more or less as they pleased, so long as they professed a belief in the Trinity and a disbelief in transubstantiation (in other words, so long as they were not Catholics, Unitarians, or Deists).

Each English colony in America was founded with its own religious focus, but some denominations held much in common with others. For instance Congregationalists, Presbyterians, and Separationists (who had very similar creeds), members of the German and Dutch Reformed churches, and Baptists could all be classified as Calvinists, and agreed on many fundamental doctrines. Anglicans, on the other hand, were *not* Calvinists and spiritually speaking had little in common with the holders of that creed. Where Calvinists had a strong conviction of original sin and a belief that salvation comes through faith rather than works, and imposed stern sumptuary laws, the not-very-zealous Anglicans saw religion more as a way of ordering and controlling society than as the very purpose of society. Quakers were in a category of their own: the Society of Friends, which had begun in England in the 1640s, espoused a primitive form of Christianity without creed, sacraments, or paid clergy, and practiced a spiritual exercise that stressed an inner search for God without clerical mediation.

The most overweeningly pious sects were the Presbyterians, Separatists, and Congregationalists. Those Puritans and "Pilgrim Fathers" we were taught to revere in our schooldays were in fact fanatically religious men whose intolerance made them anathema to people of other denominations. In the words of the historian Frank Lambert,

> The Holy Commonwealth was not intended for everyone, not even for all Christians. Of course, Catholics or "papists" were

unwelcome, but so were other Protestants, including Anglicans, Quakers, and Baptists. To Puritans, intolerance in the name of Christian purity was not only defensible but mandatory for a covenanted people. In Massachusetts, religious freedom was defined as freedom from error. Such a stance soon earned them bad press in England. Rather than extending toleration to those of different religious convictions, the Puritans persecuted dissenters in their midst just as they had been persecuted as English Dissenters.

The Massachusetts Bay colonists not only adhered to the Calvinistic doctrine of salvation by faith, they also, perhaps contradictorily, thought that spiritual election could be demonstrated only through what they called a "conversion experience." This was thought rather weird by their contemporaries—how could one know what God had supposedly preordained? But the tradition of the conversion experience continued, surviving today in modern evangelical Christians' stress on being "saved" or "born again."

The Puritans' colorful history has perhaps given them a disproportionate historical weight. It is important to remember that they never constituted a majority in the American colonies and even in their own day were seen as a sort of lunatic fringe by the Anglicans and other denominations. Captain John Smith of Virginia dismissed the separatist Plymouth Colony as "a fooles Paradise," and plenty of his contemporaries agreed with him.

One Massachusetts Bay resident who found himself unable to stomach the colony's intolerant policies was Roger Williams, a minister and early advocate of religious toleration. Well in advance of John Locke, Williams's *The Bloudy Tenet of Persecution* (1644) advocated the separation of church and state:

> But as the Civill Magistrate hath his charge of the bodies and goods of the subject: So have the spirituall Officers, Governours and overseers of Christ's City or Kingdome, the

charge of their souls, and soule safety: Hence that charge of
Paul before Timothy [1 Timothy 5:20]. Them that sinne
rebuke before all, that others may learn to fear. This is in the
Church of Christ a spirituall meanes for the healing of a soule
that hath sinned, or taken infection, and for the preventing of
the infecting of others, that others may learne to feare, etc.

Anticipating (though in Christian terms) Enlightenment ideals
of religious freedom, Williams stated his belief that civic virtue is unconnected with religion, and that religious toleration tends to promote a community's material prosperity. Conscience cannot be compelled: "Who hath not found a pallace a prison," he asked, "when
forc't to keepe within it?"

Constantly at odds with the Massachusetts authorities, Williams
repaired to nearby Narragansett Bay where he purchased land from
local Indian tribes and named his settlement Providence. Here there
was no established religion, and all Christian sects operated on an
equal basis. Magistrates were given authority only over civil matters
and were not allowed to interfere with religion. Other towns being
founded in the area, the colony of Rhode Island was given a charter
by Charles II in 1663. All citizens who professed Christianity were
assured full political rights, though these were not yet extended to
non-Christians.

Pennsylvania was founded on similarly utopian lines. Here the
Quaker William Penn, who had been imprisoned in England for
preaching, launched a "Holy Experiment" by which Christians of
every denomination were recruited to join an inclusive community in
which they would enjoy full toleration. With this plan in view, in 1681
Penn obtained a charter for the colony from Charles II.

The Holy Experiment seized the world's imagination, with political and religious philosophers praising Penn, his colony, and its
capital city of Brotherly Love. It was a noble idea, but as with so
many utopias the reality in Pennsylvania fell far short of its founder's

ideals. Tensions soon arose between the majority Quakers and the other denominations, not so much on religious lines as on political ones, with legislative power and influence continually at issue. The political arena in Pennsylvania turned out to be one of the most contentious in colonial America, with the various religious sects quickly morphing into political parties. The Holy Experiment was not an unqualified success; still, it did shift the focus of discord from the religious to the political, an achievement in its own right.

In the eighteenth century, then, this is how the American colonies stood: Anglicanism was the established religion in Virginia, Maryland, Delaware, North Carolina, South Carolina, Georgia, and New York (though much of that state was inhabited by members of the Dutch Reformed church). Massachusetts, Connecticut, and New Hampshire were Congregationalist; Pennsylvania, New Jersey, and Rhode Island had no established churches but numerous sects living more or less in harmony.

The Great Awakening of the 1740s had a cataclysmic effect on the colonies' religious, and subsequently social, organization. This evangelical movement was spread by itinerant proselytizers who traveled throughout the colonies preaching the Gospel. The arrival from England in 1739 of George Whitefield, a religious genius who brought the ministry out of the pulpit and into the streets and fields, was a key event in American colonial history. Espousing a theology of regeneration and salvation very much along the lines of our modern "born again" evangelism, Whitefield and the other itinerants challenged America's traditional and established churches with an inclusive populism. The "New Lights," as they were called, stressed the individual nature of conversion and the worshiper's personal relationship with God, independent of orthodox religious rites.

These New Lights were especially successful in the South, where the Episcopal (Anglican) church was controlled by the monied elite and the uneducated masses felt powerless. There, dissenting sects like Baptists and Methodists now began to proliferate, and soon their adherents were outnumbering the Episcopalians, which is one of the reasons Virginia would eventually find itself in the forefront of the struggle for religious freedom. Disenfranchised slaves, too, were drawn to the New Lights' promise of personal and spiritual autonomy in the sight of God—a direct contrast to the Episcopalian setup, where the church was ruled, it seemed, by the gentry rather than by their Savior.

The Great Awakening, then, was a movement that appealed largely to the poor and the unlettered. The educated classes on the other hand, while not untouched by these currents, were by mid-century beginning to move in a different direction, paying less attention to inspirational preachers than to inspiring philosophers like Locke and Shaftesbury. Deism was rapidly gaining strength among the intelligentsia; so were latitudinarianism and Unitarianism, two other liberal creeds.

Latitudinarianism was a movement that had begun among seventeenth-century theologians in England. While latitudinarians supported the Church of England, they practiced tolerance for other sects and dismissed such things as doctrine, liturgy, and church organization and leadership as "things indifferent." The latitudinarian position was popularized in America through the sermons of John Tillotson, whom the Founding Fathers often quoted with approval; we find Abigail Adams, for example, referring to "our favorite Dr. Tillotson" when writing to her husband. Tillotson preached that "Religion and happiness, our duty and our interest, are really but one and the same thing considered under several notions." God and Providence, he believed along with the deists, were essentially benign.

> If an apostle, or an angel from heaven, teach any doctrine
> which plainly overthrows the goodness and justice of God, let
> him be accursed. For every man hath a greater assurance that
> God is good and just than he can have of any subtle
> speculations about predestination and the doctrines of God.

This was reducing religion to its most basic elements, a quality latitudinarianism held in common with deism.

This was true, too, of Unitarianism, another religious movement that had developed in England during the theologically troubled seventeenth century. Unitarians believed that there was one God only, and they rejected the concept of the Trinity; Jesus they saw as a moral teacher but not divine. Unitarian doctrines, in fact, still today are so few that many more orthodox Christians refuse to acknowledge that Unitarians are Christians at all. (H. L. Mencken facetiously remarked that Unitarianism "is not a kind of Christianity at all, but simply a mattress for skeptical Christians to fall on.") Jefferson and Adams both formally identified themselves as Unitarians late in life.

Unitarianism and deism had much in common, as we can see by this excerpt from the 1759 Dudleian lecture at Harvard, delivered by Ebenezer Gay, a precursor of Unitarianism.

> The manifest Absurdity of any Doctrine, is a stronger
> Argument that it is not of God, than any other Evidence can
> be that it is. . . . To say, in Defense of any religious Tenets,
> reduced to Absurdity, that the Perfections of God, his
> Holiness, Justice, Goodness, are quite different Things in
> Him, from what, in an infinitely lower Degree, they are in
> Men, is to overthrow all Religion both natural and revealed;
> and make our Faith, as well as Reason, vain.

The chief proponent of Unitarianism during the eighteenth century was the scientist Dr. Joseph Priestley, the discoverer of oxygen, who was eventually hounded out of his native England for giving a frank account of his religous opinions and was compelled to emigrate to America. He was friends with several of the Founding Fathers, including Franklin, Jefferson, and Adams. All these men were avid readers of his books, particularly *An History of the Corruptions of Christianity* (1782), *An History of Early Opinions concerning Jesus*

Christ, compiled from Original Writers; proving that the Christian Church was at first Unitarian (1786), and *Letters to a Philosophical Unbeliever* (1787). Priestley grouped the following as untrue "corruptions" of Christianity: "a trinity of persons in the godhead, original sin, arbitrary predestination, atonement for the sins of men by the death of Christ, and (which has perhaps been as great a cause of infidelity as any other) the doctrine of the plenary inspiration of the scriptures." Jefferson was a particular disciple of Priestley, claiming that Priestley's writings were "the basis of my own faith."

Priestley took a Lockean view of the role of religion in government: that is, that the two should be kept separate.

> I have even no doubt, but that, as Christianity was promulgated, and prevailed in the world, without any aid from civil power, it will, when it shall have recovered its pristine purity, and its pristine vigour, entirely disengage itself from such an unnatural *alliance* as it is at present fettered with, and that our posterity will even look back with astonishment at the infatuation of their ancestors, in imagining that things so wholly different from each other as *Christianity* and *civil power,* had any natural connection.

Deism, latitudinarianism, and Unitarianism had an enormous influence on the Founding Fathers. Many others apart from the six discussed in this book became freethinkers of one sort or another. Gouverneur Morris, for instance, the author of the Preamble to the Constitution, was a deist *bon vivant* who owed his philosophy more to Horace (in the opinion of his biographer, Richard Brookhiser) than to Jesus—"an irreligious and profane man," according to the stern Roger Sherman of Connecticut, but one who stayed true to his Stoic beliefs. "The incidents of pleasure and pain are scattered more equally than is generally imagined," Morris observed. "The cards are dealt with fairness. What remains is patiently to play the game, and then to sleep."

Ethan Allen, the famous revolutionary and guerrilla leader, was violently outspoken in his 1784 book *Reason the Only Oracle of Man or a Compendious System of Natural Religion*. He was, he said, generally "denominated a Deist, the reality of which I never disputed, being conscious I am no Christian, except mere infant baptism makes me one; and as to being a Deist, I know not strictly speaking, whether I am one or not, for I have never read their writings." He blasted forth his thoughts on fundamental Christian doctrines with small consideration for the tender sensibilities of his believing readers:

> The doctrine of the *Incarnation* itself, and the *Virgin mother*, does not merit a serious confutation and therefore is passed in silence, except the mere mention of it.

> The doctrine of the Trinity is destitute of foundation, and tends manifestly to superstition and idolatry.

> Who in the exercise of reason can believe, that Adam and Eve by eating of such a spontaneous fruit could have incurred the eternal displeasure of God, as individuals? Or that the divine vindictive justice should extend to their un-offending offspring then unborn? And sentence the human progeny to the latest posterity to ever lasting destruction?

On the atonement:

> . . . [T]here could be no justice or goodness in one being's suffering for another, nor is it at all compatible with reason to suppose, that God was the contriver of such a proposition.

Or on the Ten Commandments: such moral precepts, he said,

> were previously known to every nation under heaven, and in all probability by them as much practised as by the tribes of Israel.

And so on, for more than four hundred pages.

Another Founding Father with an axe to grind against orthodox Christianity was William Livingston, first governor of New Jersey and the chief advocate in New York for the separation of church and state. During colonial days Livingston had opposed the idea of affiliating King's College in New York (now Columbia University) with the Anglican church. If the college became a seminary of the Church of England, he wrote, it would be the "Nursery of Bigotry and Superstition.—An Engine of Persecution, Slavery and Oppression.— A Fountain whose putrid and infectious Streams will overflow the Land, and poison all our Enjoyments." Livingston's rhetoric was heartfelt. "Whenever Men have suffered their Consciences to be enslaved by their Superiors, and taken their Religion upon Trust, the World has been over-run with Superstition, and held in Fetters by a tyrannizing Juncto of civil and ecclesiastical Plunderers."

But the most outspoken of all the revolutionaries, and certainly the most shocking to his more pious contemporaries, was Thomas Paine. Paine, though an Englishman, can be counted as one of our Founding Fathers simply by virtue of his galvanizing effect on public opinion. His 1776 pamphlet *Common Sense*, which attacked the abuses of George III's government and loudly advocated American independence, was a phenomenal best-seller and inspired revolutionary unity in the colonists. Later he wrote *The Rights of Man* as a spirited defense of the French Revolution in response to Edmund Burke's criticism of its excesses.

Paine had long been a deist who grumbled against the irrationality of Christianity and its bloody and intolerant history. John Adams described hearing Paine expound against the Bible. "'The Old Testament!' said he, 'I do not believe in the Old Testament. I have had thoughts of publishing my sentiments of it, but upon deliberation I have concluded to put that off till the latter part of my life.'" Eventually Paine did turn to the task, producing in 1795 *The Age of Reason*, a bold defense of deism and an attack on Christianity, especially biblical revelation.

Whenever we read the obscene stories, the voluptuous debaucheries, the cruel and torturous executions, the unrelenting vindictiveness, with which more than half the Bible is filled, it would be more consistent that we called it the word of a demon, than the word of God. It is a history of wickedness, that has served to corrupt and brutalize mankind; and, for my own part, I sincerely detest it, as I detest every thing that is cruel.

[The New Testament's "fable"] for absurdity and extravagance is not exceeded by any thing that is to be found in the mythology of the ancients. . . . Putting aside every thing that might excite laughter by its absurdity, or detestation by its prophaneness, and confining ourselves merely to an examination of the parts, it is impossible to conceive a story more derogatory to the Almighty, more inconsistent with his wisdom, more contradictory to his power, than this story is.

I believe in one God, and no more; and I hope for happiness beyond this life.

I believe in the equality of man, and I believe that religious duties consist in doing justice, loving mercy, and endeavoring to make our fellow-creatures happy.

But lest it should be supposed that I believe many other things in addition to these, I shall, in the progress of this work, declare the things I do not believe, and my reasons for not believing them.

I do not believe in the creed professed by the Jewish church, by the Roman church, by the Greek church, by the Turkish church, by the Protestant church, nor by any church that I know of. My own mind is my own church.

All national institutions of churches, whether Jewish, Christian, or Turkish, appear to me no other than human inventions set up to terrify and enslave mankind, and monopolize power and profit.

[H]owever unwilling the partizans of the Christian system may be to believe or to acknowledge it, it is nevertheless true, that the age of ignorance commenced with the Christian system. . . . [T]he Christian system laid all waste.

Not too surprisingly, Paine stirred up tremendous wrath for holding these opinions and sharing them with the public. He was used to this, of course, and probably even enjoyed the furor; in past years he had been imprisoned in France and had narrowly escaped the same fate in England. Returning to America in 1802 he found that the climate of the times had changed and a new religiosity was sweeping the country. According to public opinion then, Paine was no longer the hero of the Revolution but merely a disreputable old infidel. Some of his friends, however, rallied round, and President Jefferson invited him to the White House, braving considerable onus from zealous Christian citizens in doing so.

Paine was a writer, not a politician, so he could afford to be far more outspoken than his friends Jefferson, Franklin, and Adams. Yet now that we can examine their private letters and papers, it is clear that these men's religious views really differed very little from Paine's, if at all.

Their ideas, like those of so many of the Founding Fathers, were incalculably influenced by the mental climate of the Enlightenment— a period lasting roughly from the 1680s to the 1790s. This mental climate had developed in response to new scientific and geographical studies of the era and in reaction to the grisly religious wars of the Reformation and the hundred years following it. Enlightenment ideas were contagious and quickly leaped across national boundaries, though political and social situations varied widely throughout Europe and the American colonies.

In many parts of the world, historical circumstances inspired thinking people to question received notions—social, political, and religious—more profoundly than they had done for centuries. England's Glorious Revolution of 1688, for instance, put an end to a long tradition of royal absolutism and created, for the first time, a constitutional monarchy and a large measure of religious toleration for its subjects. The nation quickly became a beacon of political and religious freedom, at least relatively speaking, within Europe. In France, on the other hand, the 1685 revocation of the tolerant Edict of Nantes ushered in an era of renewed religious suppression and persecution against non-Catholics, enraging the country's already disaffected intellectuals. These so-called *philosophes* were intoxicated by the great scientific discoveries of Isaac Newton, Francis Bacon, and their heirs, and found that the new science now made any literal interpretation of the Bible rather problematic.

The central Enlightenment thesis, in the wake of the Newtonian intellectual revolution, was that the universe was a comprehensible place, governed by laws which could be understood through scientific inquiry. This proposition does not seem particularly radical now but at the time it was, extremely so. Almost by definition it put biblical revelation on a very shaky footing, and it was during the Enlightenment that science and creationism embarked on the long war they are still bitterly fighting today. Christianity reeled from the blow dealt it by the Newtonian cosmogony. Suddenly the Old Testament seemed to be neither sacred history nor revealed religion, but, in the historian Peter Gay's words, "an incriminating document. It revealed, if it revealed anything, the vices of the Chosen People and the tainted sources of the Christian religion." This was a revelation that reinforced the bad impression made by religious zealots—Catholics, Puritans, doctrinaire Anglicans, and nearly every other sect—during the wars of religion that had lasted throughout the sixteenth and seventeenth centuries.

Gay goes on to outline the generally negative opinion of revealed religion that became dominant among Enlightenment intellectuals:

In its early history, its very origins, there was something unsavory about Christianity. Significantly, it flourished in an age of decadence and among the lower orders, among men and women sunk in ignorance, vice, and despair. Significantly, too, it hammered out its doctrine, its discipline and organization, amidst undignified wranglings, inane debates in endless assemblies, angry conflicts over trivial matters, mutual slanders and persecutions. Christianity claimed to bring light, hope, and truth, but its central myth was incredible, its dogma a conflation of rustic superstitions, its sacred book an incoherent collection of primitive tales, its church a cohort of servile fanatics as long as they were out of power and of despotic fanatics once they had seized control. With its triumph in the fourth century, Christianity secured the victory of infantile credulity; one by one, the lamps of learning were put out, and for centuries darkness covered the earth.

Edward Gibbon's multivolume *Decline and Fall of the Roman Empire* (1776–1788), especially its famous fifteenth and sixteenth chapters, took what had by then become the classic Enlightenment position: the nobler world of antiquity had been degraded and ultimately destroyed by Christianity, which by suppressing truth, philosophy, and science had sunk the West into centuries of darkness. Comparisons between ancient polytheism and Christian monotheism did not show the latter to advantage: polytheism was tolerant, monotheism intolerant; polytheism was easygoing, monotheism evangelical; polytheism demanded nothing from its adherents save ritual acts, while monotheism imposed all kinds of irrational rites.

The late seventeenth century witnessed a sign of the coming times in the form of biblical criticism, with secular scholars like the Dutch philosopher Spinoza and the French Pierre Bayle and

Richard Simon submitting the Bible to the same evidentiary standards that were being imposed on other ancient texts. To the intelligentsia the miracles and supernatural events in which Scripture abounds were beginning to look at best like symbols and metaphors, at worst like fantastic and superstitious inventions. And then there was the spiritual chaos of post-Reformation Europe, with its multiplicity of sects each claiming unique divine authority: Arminians, Presbyterians, Dunkers, Quakers, Anabaptists, and countless others. This situation did not exactly help reconcile the growing number of rationalists to the Christian faith.

The great age of geographical discovery, too, had presented the formerly provincial Europeans with the prospect of a wide world filled with thriving cultures, all with entirely different spiritual traditions. Educated Europe was beginning to observe its own religious practices, as well as foreign ones, with a new species of anthropological detachment. In his *Lettres persanes* (1721), for example, the Baron de Montesquieu imagined the reactions of two Persian visitors to the customs and mores of Louis XV's Paris, introducing a note of cultural and religious relativism that soon became a characteristic feature of the Enlightenment.

The two main strains in Enlightenment thought, rationalism and emancipationism, seemed to go hand in hand through much of the period, especially in the American colonies. As the Enlightenment age progressed, Christianity and its various sects became increasingly associated with systems of political oppression. England's Glorious Revolution had proved that men and women did not have to submit to any abusive monarch, even one who claimed to rule by divine right. The relationship between the governor and the governed, it now appeared, was a contractual one and in no way ordained by God.

The most important political thinker of the Enlightenment and certainly the one who had the greatest impact in America was John Locke (1632–1704), who did as much as any theorist has ever done

to loosen politics from the bonds of organized religion. Responding
to the bitter battles waged in England during his lifetime by religious dissenters seeking a measure of toleration, between 1689 and
1692 he wrote his three famous "Letters Concerning Toleration."
These documents had an incalculable influnce on our Founding Fathers, their conception of an ideal government, and the constitutional
settlement they finally reached.

In clear and absolutely uncompromising prose, Locke set out
the principles of church-state separation that the Founding Fathers
would adopt and expand on. The state, he wrote,

> seems to me to be a society of men constituted only for the
> procuring, preserving, and advancing their own civil interests.
> Civil interests I call life, liberty, health, and indolence of body;
> and the possession of outward things, such as money, lands,
> houses, furniture, and the like. It is the duty of the civil
> magistrate, by the impartial execution of equal laws, to secure
> unto all the people in general, and to every one of his subjects
> in particular the just possession of these things belonging to
> this life.

And there, in Locke's scheme, governmental authority ends. It
should be restricted to purely civil interests. "Now that the whole jurisdiction of the magistrate reaches only to these civil concernments,
. . . and that it neither can nor ought in any manner to be extended
to the salvation of souls." Religion, so long as its practice brings injury neither to the bodies nor to the property of citizens, is by its very
nature wholly outside civil jurisdiction.

> If a Roman Catholic believe that to be really the body of
> Christ, which another man calls bread, he does no injury
> thereby to his neighbor. If a Jew do not believe the New
> Testament to be the word of God, he does not thereby alter
> anything in men's civil rights. If a heathen doubt of both

Testaments, he is not therefore to be punished as a pernicious citizen. The power of the magistrate and the estates of the people may be equally secure whether any man believe these things or no. . . .

(Thomas Jefferson, in other words, was only paraphrasing Locke when he scandalously wrote that "it does me no injury for my neighbor to say there are twenty gods, or no God. It neither picks my pocket, nor breaks my leg.")

Locke continued in authoritative tones:

[T]he business of laws is not to provide for the truth of opinions, but for the safety and security of the commonwealth, and of every particular man's goods and person. And so it ought to be. For the truth certainly would do well enough if she were once left to shift for herself.

Again we hear Jefferson's echo, this time in his Virginia Statute for Religious Freedom: ". . . truth is great and will prevail if left to herself, . . . she is the proper and sufficient antagonist to error, and has nothing to fear from the conflict. . . . "

Churches, Locke insisted, were purely free and voluntary bodies. "Nobody is born a member of any church. . . . A church, then, is a society of members voluntarily uniting to [worship]. . . . " Any person is free to enter a church, and "why should it not be as free for him to go out as it was to enter?" Government, emphatically, should leave religion alone, and religion should return the courtesy.

. . . [S]eeing one man does not violate the right of another by his erronious opinions and undue manner of worship, nor is his perdition any prejudice to another man's affairs, therefore, the care of each man's salvation belongs only to himself. . . . [N]obody else is concerned in it, nor can receive any prejudice from his conduct therein. . . .

But if the law indeed be concerning things that lie not within the verge of the magistrate's authority (as, for example, that the people, or any party amongst them, should be compelled to embrace a strange religion, and join in the worship and ceremonies of another church), men are not in these cases obliged by that law, against their consciences.

All these sentiments would be passionately seconded by Thomas Jefferson and James Madison: the first part of the Declaration of Independence, in fact, bristles with Lockean phrases and ideas. Through disciples like Jefferson, Madison, Franklin, John and Samuel Adams, Patrick Henry, and James Otis, Locke's philosophy of government made its way wholesale into the American system. Ours is, or at least was originally designed to be, a Lockean state.

In Britain, Locke's theories were incorporated into the the liberal, or Whig, philosophy of government espoused by the political philosophers who would influence the American Founding Fathers in their turn: Henry St. John, 1st Viscount Bolingbroke; Samuel Clarke; James Burgh; Anthony Ashley Cooper, 3rd Earl of Shaftesbury; Adam Smith; and the great philosopher of the Scottish Enlightenment, David Hume. Shaftesbury's *Characteristics of Men, Manners, Opinions, Times, etc.* (1699) indicates the direction in which thought was then tending: religion, and specifically Christianity in its various sects, was no longer looked on as the indispensable and infallible guide for our every action but as a separate and sometimes irrelevant preoccupation—or even, indeed, mere superstition. Shaftesbury spoke of religious impulses as "mental eruptions," "panic," or a "humor" in mankind that "of necessity must have vent" if it is not to create social disturbances. The ancients, he believed, had solved this perennial problem admirably:

It was heretofore the wisdom of some wise nations to let people be fools as much as they pleased, and never to punish seriously what deserved only to be laughed at, and was, after all, best cured by that innocent remedy. . . . They are certainly as ill physicians in the body-politic who would needs be tampering with these mental eruptions; and under the specious pretense of healing this itch of superstition, and saving souls from the contagion of enthusiasm, should set all nature in an uproar, and turn a few innocent carbuncles into an inflammation and moral gangrene.

Shaftesbury's use of language here tells us a great deal about his attitude toward religious zeal, an attitude that would come down to the Founding Fathers: the "itch of superstition" and other such "mental eruptions," spread by "contagion," should be healed by the "innocent remedy" of laughter.

The antidote to "superstition," Shaftesbury said, was philosophy—what we would now define simply as education—which had been sorely lacking in strict religious communities. Superstition could be fought not only with "wit" and "raillery" but with serious study, for the person who sincerely seeks historical and philosophical knowledge will be exposed to countless other belief systems with equal—or equally ridiculous—claims to infallibility. Shaftesbury implicitly denied all such claims; religion, he insisted, was contingent upon geography and time. "He who is now an orthodox Christian," he wrote, in which of course he included the vast majority of his own countrymen, "would have been infallibly as true a Mussulman, or as errant a heretic, had his birth been in another place."

Shaftesbury argued persuasively to the people who objected—as some people always do—that religious liberty might go too far. His observations on the subject anticipated points that would later be made by the more libertarian among the Founding Fathers:

'Tis true, this liberty may seem to run too far. We may perhaps be said to make ill use of it. So every one will say, when he himself is touched, and his opinion freely examined. But who shall be judge of what may be freely examined and what may not? Where liberty may be used and where it may not? What remedy shall we prescribe to this in general? Can there be a better than from that liberty itself which is complained of?

Who, in short, will guard the guardians?

David Hume's thought would eventually lead him into a skepticism too profound and disturbing for the Founding Fathers to pursue; they were, after all, practical men concerned with creating a practical government, and had perforce to deal with a religious citizenry. Nevertheless his work had a great influence on the intellectual climate in which they lived and which colored their thoughts on human nature and, by extension, human society and government. Hume's widely read *Enquiry Concerning Human Understanding* (1748) amounted to an all-out assault on revealed religion. In the chapter "Of Miracles," he wrote that Christianity's dependence on miracles to secure its *bona fides* did not speak well for it, and remarked in passing that "It forms a strong presumption against all supernatural and miraculous relations, that they are observed chiefly to abound among ignorant and barbarous nations." He seems to have included, among such "barbarous nations," those into which the authors of both the Old and New Testaments were born. ". . . [T]he *Christian Religion* not only was at first attended with miracles, but even at this day cannot be believed by any reasonable person without one," he wrote in his famous debunking of miraculous events. He urged his readers to scrutinize religious texts as open-mindedly as they would any other: "If we take in our hand any volume; of divinity or school metaphysics, for instance; let us ask, *Does it contain any abstract reasoning concerning quantity or number?* No. *Does it contain any experimental reasoning concerning matter of fact and existence?* No. Commit it then to the flames: for it can contain nothing but sophistry and illusion."

In *An Enquiry Concerning Human Understanding* and *The Origin of Polytheism*, Hume theorized that the religious impulse derives primarily from fear. Like Machiavelli, he believed fear to serve as a more powerful force than love or any other positive motivation. "Agitated by hopes and fears—especially the latter, men scrutinize, with a trembling curiosity, the course of future causes and examine the various and contrary events of human life." The more primitive the society, the more precarious life is and hence the more religious, or the more superstitious—Hume used the terms almost interchangeably—the people tend to be.

Hume effectively attacked the popular practice of "proving" God's existence from the design of the universe, and went on, in "The Natural History of Religion" (1757) to state his belief that ultimate truth is impossible to grasp—in words that the aged John Adams would all but repeat three-quarters of a century later.

> The whole is a riddle, an aenigma, an inexplicable mystery. Doubt, uncertainty, suspense of judgment appear the only result of our most accurate scrutiny, concerning this subject. But such is the frailty of human reason, and such the irresistible contagion of opinion, that even this deliberate doubt could scarcely be upheld; did we not enlarge our view, and opposing one species of superstition to another, set them a quarreling; while we ourselves, during their fury and contention, happily make our escape into the calm, though obscure regions of philosophy.

Far from concluding that a lack of religion would create a moral vacuum, Hume appeared to believe that the moral sense could function perfectly well in the absence of dogma. "I see not what bad consequences follow, in the present age, from the character [reputation] of an infidel; especially if a man's conduct be in other respects irreproachable," he wrote to a friend. "What is your opinion?" Jefferson, among other prominent Americans of the period, agreed with him here, and so did other luminaries of the Scottish Enlightenment, including the great liberal economist Adam Smith.

In his *Theory of Moral Sentiments* (1759), Smith located the moral sense in a human capacity for empathy that is innate and independent of religion, and constructed an ethical system from elements derived from Stoic, Epicurean, Platonic, and more modern philosophy. "Popular superstition and enthusiasm"—that is, religious zeal—he considered a poison that should be purged through the study of science and philosophy. As with the free market theory of his 1776 *The Wealth of Nations*, he saw monopoly as harmful, in religion as well as in earthly commodities:

> [Z]eal must be altogether innocent where the society is divided into two or three hundred, or perhaps into as many thousand small sects, of which no one would be considerable enough to disturb the public tranquility. The teachers of each sect, seeing themselves surrounded on all sides with more adversaries than friends, would be obliged to [exercise] . . . moderation.

Smith was proposing that in a state of pure religious freedom, no one sect could collect enough adherents to gain ascendency over the others, and that each would hence be equally free. This is exactly the position that James Madison, among other American founders, would adopt when it came to the church/state settlement in the new nation.

The retreat from traditional Christianity among Britain's educated class resulted in the growth of a movement known as deism. Deists believed, briefly, that there was one, and only one, God (or Supreme Being, or Deity, or whatever one might want to call him); that that God had created the world but did not take an active role in our day-to-day doings; that He was benign and undemanding, unlike the jealous Yahweh of the Old Testament or Allah of the Koran; that nature was governed by physical laws that could be understood through reason; that ethical laws, equally, were also indicated by reason and nature; and that Providence was benign. Deists did not believe in the divinity of Jesus Christ, the existence of hell, or revelation.

The English deists flourished in the early to mid-eighteenth century. Key texts—books with which the well-educated Founding Fathers were familiar—included John Toland's *Christianity Not Mysterious* (1696), Samuel Clarke's *Discourse Concerning the Being and Attributes of God* (1704–1705), and Matthew Tindal's *Christianity as Old as Creation* (1730).

These men's influence in their own country was limited, but their ideas flourished in the American colonies: Tom Paine, Ethan Allen, Thomas Jefferson, Benjamin Franklin, John Adams (later in life), Gouverneur Morris, and possibly George Washington, among many others, were deists. Generally speaking, deists considered Jesus Christ a great philosopher but not divine or divinely inspired. They rejected out of hand the innumerable dogma that had been grafted onto Christ's simple message ever since Saint Paul began his ministry in the first century. The basic principles of deism made their way into the Unitarian church, where they still thrive today.

The eighteenth-century American theologian Jonathan Edwards described deists as blasphemers and heretics. Voicing the standard Calvinist view of the deists, he complained that they had

> Wholly cast off the Christian religion, and are professed infidels. They are not like the Heretics, Arians, Socinians, and others, who own the Scriptures to be the word of God, and hold the Christian religion to be the true religion, but only deny these and these fundamental doctrines of the Christian religion; they deny the whole Christian religion. Indeed they own the being of a God; but they deny that Christ was the son of God, and say he was a mere cheat; and so they say all the prophets and apostles were; and they deny the whole Scripture. They deny that any of it is the word of God. They deny any revealed religion, or any word of God at all; and say that God has given mankind no other light to walk by but their own reason.

If these blandishments are true, then they are true of many of our revered Founding Fathers.

Eighteenth-century England was a relatively liberal society, a constitutional monarchy in which certain basic individual rights were protected by law. This was not the case in France, where an absolute monarch still resided at Versailles along with a powerful nobility that was accountable to no one but themselves and whose activities had fossilized into meaningless ritual and ceremony. Political and religious dissidents were regularly prosecuted and locked up; civil liberties were nonexistent. Hence French freethinking took on a much more passionate, violent tone than the English variety. In the salons of the Paris *philosophes* the Catholic creed was openly and scornfully rejected, and outspoken atheism flourished. Voltaire, Montesquieu, Diderot, d'Alembert, d'Holbach, Helvétius—all these men, the most celebrated thinkers in pre-Revolutionary France, repudiated the Catholic church and professed either deism or atheism. In the words of Voltaire, the greatest popularizer of Enlightenment ideas and a huge influence on Benjamin Franklin and Thomas Jefferson, "I conclude all my letters by saying, *Ecrasez l'infame*" [Crush the infamous]. By "*l'infame*" Voltaire meant the Catholic church. "Every sensible man," he wrote, "every honorable man, must hold the Christian sect in horror."

Voltaire claimed to be a deist rather than an atheist, as many of his friends were. Witnessing a beautiful sunrise on a hilltop at his country estate, for example, he famously cried "I believe, I believe in you! Almighty God, I believe!" but then added, "As for Monsieur, the son, and Madame, his mother, that's quite another matter." When challenged in his deist faith, he defended it as the only *sensible* option. "Men are blind," he said, "to prefer an absurd and sanguinary creed, supported by executioners and surrounded by fiery faggots, a creed which can only be approved by those to whom it gives power and riches, a particular creed only accepted in a small part of the world—to a simple and universal religion." It was the "simple and universal" aspect of deism that appealed to the Founding Fathers, who were faced with the daunting task of joining a population of enormous religious diversity into a political whole.

Voltaire objected loudly to critics who complained that the removal of Christianity would leave a theological and moral vacuum. "What!" he exclaimed. "A ferocious animal has sucked the blood of my family; I tell you to get rid of that beast, and you ask me, What shall we put in its place!" Morality, he believed, was natural to man, its principles clearly written in nature and nature's laws. Deism, or "natural religion," he defined as the moral system broadly accepted by the entire human race.

The following excerpt from Voltaire's *Philosophical Dictionary* is worth quoting at length because it so exactly illustrates the attitudes of the American Founding Fathers on the subject of sectarian strife.

SECT

Every sect, of every kind, is a rallying point for doubt and error. Scotist, Thomist, Realist, Nominalist, Papist, Calvinist, Molinist, and Jansenist are only pseudonyms.

There are no sects in geometry. One does not speak of a Euclidean, an Archimedean. When the truth is evident, it is impossible for parties and factions to arise. There has never been a dispute as to whether there is daylight at noon. The branch of astronomy which determines the course of the stars and the return of eclipses being once known, there is no dispute among astronomers.

In England one does not say: "I am a Newtonian, a Lockian, a Halleyan." Why? Those who have read cannot refuse their assent to the truths taught by these three great men. The more Newton is revered, the less do people style themselves Newtonians; this word supposes that there are anti-Newtonians in England. Maybe we still have a few Cartesians

in France, but only because Descartes' system is a tissue of
erronious and ridiculous speculations. . . .

You are a Mohammedan; therefore there are people who
are not; therefore you might well be wrong.

What would be the true religion if Christianity did not
exist? The religion in which there were no sects, the religion in
which all minds were necessarily in agreement.

Well, to what dogma do all minds agree? To the worship of
a God, and to honesty. All the philosophers of the world who
have had a religion have said in all ages, "There is a God, and
one must be just." There, then, is the universal religion
established in all ages and throughout mankind. The point in
which they all agree is therefore true, and the systems through
which they differ are therefore false. . . .

When Zoroaster, Hermes, Orpheus, Minos, and all the
great men say: "Let us worship God, and let us be just,"
nobody laughs. But everyone hisses the man who claims that
one cannot please God unless one is holding a cow's tail when
one dies; or the man who wants one to have the end of one's
prepuce cut off; or the man who consecrates crocodiles and
onions; or the man who attaches eternal salvation to dead men's
bones carried under one's shirt, or to a plenary indulgence
which may be bought at Rome for two and an half *sous*. . . .

Sect and *error* are synonymous. You are a Peripatetic and I
a Platonist; we are therefore both wrong; for you combat Plato
only because his fantasies have revolted you, while I am
alienated from Aristotle only because it seems to me that he
does not know what he is talking about. If one or other had
demonstrated the truth, there would be a sect no longer. To
declare oneself for the opinion of one or the other is to take
sides in a civil war. There are no sects in mathematics, in
experimental physics. A man who examines the relations
between a cone and a sphere is not of the sect of Archimedes;

he who sees that the square of the hypotenuse of a right-angled triable is equal to the square of the two other sides is not of the sect of Pythagoras.

When you say that the blood circulates, that the air is heavy, that the sun's rays are pencils of seven refrangible rays, you are not either of the sect of Harvey, or the sect of Torricelli, or the sect of Newton; you merely agree with the truth as demonstrated by them, and the entire world will always be of your opinion.

This is the character of truth: it is of all time, it is for all men, it has only to show itself to be recognized, and one cannot argue against it. A long dispute means that *both parties are wrong.*

In the detailed correspondence they carried on in old age, Jefferson and Adams said precisely the same thing, and it seems impossible that Jefferson did not have Voltaire's words in mind as he wrote. Pressed to define his personal creed, Adams said that in spite of sixty years of theological reading and study, his religion was "contained in four short words, 'Be just and good.'" Jefferson responded, "The result of our fifty or sixty years of religious reading, in the four words, 'Be just and good,' is that in which all our inquiries must end, as the riddles of all priesthoods end in four more, *'ubi panis, ibi deus'* [where there is bread, there is God]. What all agree in, is probably right. What no two agree in, most probably wrong."

Voltaire did much to popularize Locke's ideas of religious tolerance, and his writings on this subject obviously influenced the philosophy of the Constitution and are reflected in the writings of James Madison, often called "the Father of the Constitution." (Madison was ferociously studious and had steeped himself in all the important political philosophers, both ancient and modern.) The following excerpts from Voltaire's *Philosophical Dictionary* can be seen as the clear stepping stone between Locke and Madison.

It has been said before, and it must be said again: if you have
two religions in your land, the two will cut each other's throats;
but if you have thirty religions, they will dwell in peace. Look
at the Great Turk [the Ottoman Sultan]. He governs Guebres,
Banians, Greek Christians, Nestorians, Romans. The first who
tried to stir up tumult would be impaled; and everyone is at
peace. . . . Discord is the great ill of mankind, and tolerance is
the only remedy for it.

Our soul acts internally. Internal acts are thought, volition,
inclinations, acquiescence in certain truths. All these acts are
above coercion, and are within the ecclesiastical minister's
sphere only in so far as he must instruct, but never command.

The soul also acts externally. External actions are under
the civil law. Here coercion may have a place; temporal or
corporal penalties maintain the law by punishing those who
infringe it.

Obedience to ecclesiastical order must consequently always
be free and voluntary: no other should be possible. Submission
to civil order, on the other hand, may be compulsory and
compelled.

The French *philosophes* felt that Locke's concept of religious "toleration," in which there was an established state religion which tolerated dissident sects, did not go far enough, and they discussed the
qualitative difference between full religious freedom, with no established church, and mere toleration. The revolutionary Comte de
Mirabeau, for instance, protested that "The most unlimited liberty
of religion is in my eyes a right so sacred that to express it by the
word 'toleration' seems to me itself a sort of tyranny, since the authority which tolerates might also not tolerate." This argument
would be taken up by Washington, Adams, Jefferson, and Madison,
who advocated full freedom with no established religion at all (rather
than mere toleration). After many tussles they were successful in this

struggle, and the rights embodied in Jefferson's Virginia Statute for Religious Freedom were eventually incorporated into the Constitution and the Bill of Rights.

The concept of "natural rights" and "natural law" that did so much to inform the American Declaration of Independence and, ultimately, the Constitution, flourished during the Enlightenment. As Voltaire said, "the eternal and immutable truths . . . are founded on natural law and the necessary order of society." Early Enlightenment legal thinkers like Hugo Grotius and Samuel Pufendorf, as well as John Locke, had spread the concept of natural law through the educated elite, and by the time the founding generation was of university age these ideas made up an important part of the curriculum: at Harvard, for example, Jean-Jacques Burlamaqui's *Principles of Natural Law* was a standard text, read there by James Otis, John Hancock, and John and Samuel Adams. Hand-in-hand with the idea of natural law—"Nature and Nature's God"—was the definition of "virtue"— an extremely important concept to the founding generation—as public and civic rather than as private and devotional. In the words of Claude-Adrien Helvétius in his *Treatise on Man*:

> He is virtuous who promotes the prosperity of his fellow-citizens: the word virtue always indicates the idea of some public utility. . . . [W]hat are monks in general? Idle and litigious men, dangerous to society, and whose vicinity is to be dreaded. Their conduct proves that there is nothing in common between religion and virtue.

Virtue was returning, in other words, to its classical, Roman meaning and shedding the association with piety it had assumed during the long Christian era. Henceforth, Enlightenment thinkers believed, virtue would be defined by someone like George Washington, a man of civic merit rather than showy piety. When his contemporaries wished to praise Washington they compared him with pagan rather than Christian models, the favorite being the Roman general Cincinnatus.

Many of the *philosophes* took the position, radical at that time, that virtue and morality stood in no need of religion as a prop. Rousseau, Condorcet, and Jefferson believed that everyone was born with a natural moral sense; some took this further, claiming that religion actively hampered the moral instincts endowed by nature. As the Baron d'Holbach wrote, "I feel, and another feels like me; this is the foundation of all morals. . . ." The Golden Rule, in fact. And there was then no reason an atheist should not be just as moral as anyone else.

> It is asked what motives an Atheist can have to do good?
> [d'Holbach wrote.] The motive to please himself and his
> fellow-creatures; to live happily and peaceably; to gain the
> affection and esteem of men, whose existence and dispositions
> are much more sure and known, than those of a being
> impossible to be known. "Can he who fears not the gods, fear
> anything?" He can fear men; he can fear contempt, dishonor,
> the punishment and vengeance of the laws; in short, he can
> fear himself, and the remorse felt by all those who are
> conscious of having incurred or merited the hatred of their
> fellow-creatures.

This sentiment is echoed again and again in the writings of the Founding Fathers. Virtue brings happiness, vice unhappiness, both to the individual subject and to society in general. The nature of virtue is not mysterious, to be comprehended only through Christian revelation; it is clearly evident in nature and discernible through the exercise of reason.

The conscious creation of a new republic on a strong, centralized legal basis was a more or less unprecedented project in 1787. It involved the best legal minds of the thirteen former colonies, most of whom were deeply versed in Enlightenment political philosophy. All of the principles we have discussed in this chapter were incorporated into the new nation's legal code and stated philosophy. The result seemed to be, at least in the eyes of the Enlightenment thinkers who witnessed it, a resounding success. In the opinion of the Marquis de Condorcet, America was of all nations "the most enlightened, the freest and the least burdened by prejudices," and the rights guaranteed by the Constitution were natural rights that should be enjoyed by all humanity. Denis Diderot, who had bitterly protested against ecclesiastical rule in his *Encyclopédie*, praised America as "offering all the inhabitants of Europe an asylum against fanaticism and tyranny."

The United States of America was planned, then, as an Enlightenment ideal, an asylum against fanaticism in which everyone would be free to worship—or *not* to worship—according to his or her own inclinations. But even as the delegates to the Constitutional Convention were busy with their task, the clash between Enlightenment thought and traditional power structures in the form of church and crown were coming to a crisis in France. In 1789 the outbreak of the French Revolution seemed a moment of hope in which both secular and ecclesiastical tyrants would be trampled underfoot and Reason at last enthroned in her rightful place. But the violence in France soon spun out of control, and the world watched in horror as self-defined "rationalists" swiftly transformed themselves into a brand-new type of tyrant, ideological rather than religious.

Reaction set in everywhere. As Napoleon's armies devastated huge portions of Europe, France's revolutionary rage began to be linked in popular opinion with the philosophical climate that had led to the Revolution—the political radicalism and religious skepticism of the French *philosophes*. This anarchy, people reasoned, was divine punishment for the people's abandonment of piety and tradition. The entire Enlightenment project began to be looked upon with grave suspicion, and in the early days of the nineteenth century a new wave of conservatism and religiosity swept over the Western world.

In the long run the Enlightenment became so intimately linked with the French Revolution and its outcome that it obscured the countless other effects this great intellectual movement has had on all our lives. Today even anti-Enlightenment religious fundamentalists avail themselves of modern medicine and technology: they take aspirin, drive cars, use the internet, all of which are the product of scientific methods pioneered by Enlightenment thinkers and polished by their successors. And what about the ideal of freedom, the principle that in America has served as a beacon for both the left and the right, the religious and the secular, for the past three hundred years? This has become such a fundamental part of our thinking that we have all but forgotten its origin as an Enlightenment project. But in fact no one before that era ever considered individual autonomy to be a "natural" right.

In spite of these facts, the entire Enlightenment worldview has been consistently attacked not only from the faith-based right but from the intellectual left as well. The Enlightenment belief in reason and the perfectibility of man has been severely challenged first by the French Revolution and the Napoleonic Wars, then by the grisly crimes of the Nazis and other totalitarian regimes in the twentieth century; the theories of Freud, so highly influential over the last hundred years, indicated hidden abysses in human nature that have been borne out all too convincingly by political events. Man, recent philosophers have claimed, is a far darker creature than the eighteenth-century optimists were ready to admit. Dominant thinkers such as Michel Foucault, Jean-François Lyotard, and Theodor Adorno have debunked the Enlightenment ideal of "progress" as a specious myth.

But it is almost certainly more correct as well as more practical to look at the Enlightenment as, in the formulation of Jürgen Habermas, an "unfinished project." The advent of violent revolution in France and the subsequent political and religious reaction had the effect of retarding the momentum of the movement all over Europe and America. This created a social tension that has never been resolved. Today the heirs of the Enlightenment continually struggle with the heirs of their reactionary foes, and the difficulty of settling issues such as stem-cell research and "intelligent design" instruction in public schools is the unhappy result.

But critics of the Enlightenment, in looking at it as a monolithic programme of unjustified optimism, have too often misunderstood its nature. The Enlightenment had faith in science. Science is not merely an array of debatable facts, as its religious critics claim (i.e., "Evolution is true"), but a series of hypotheses that are continually subject to empirical investigation, change, and refinement through inquiry (i.e., "The theory of evolution is a tool that helps us understand science and history; it can and should be modified and perfected through continued experimentation"). In the words of H. G. Wells, "Science is neither knowledge nor speculation. It is criticism ending in wisdom." This is the true spirit of the Enlightenment—a spirit that is now under threat, exactly as it was two centuries ago.

_____

Two Letters from Jefferson on the Common Law and Christianity

I. EXCERPT FROM A LETTER FROM THOMAS JEFFERSON TO JOHN ADAMS, JANUARY 24, 1814:

You ask me if I have ever seen the work of J. W. Goethen's Schristen. Never. Nor did the question ever occur to me before Where did we get the ten commandments? The book indeed gives them to us verbatim. But where did it get them? For itself tells us they were written by the finger of god on tables of stone, which were destroyed by Moses: it specifies those on the 2nd. set of tables in different form and substance, but still without saying how the others were recovered. But the whole history of these books is so defective and doubtful that it seems vain to attempt minute enquiry into it: and such tricks have plaid with their text, and with the texts of other books relating to them, that we have a right, from that cause, to entertain much doubt what parts of them are genuine. In the New testament there is internal evidence that parts of it have proceeded from an extraordinary man; and that other parts are the fabric of very inferior minds. It is as easy to separate those parts, as to pick diamonds from dunghills. The matter of the first was such as would be preserved in the memory of the hearers, and handed on by tradition for a long time; and the latter such stuff as might be gathered up, for imbedding it, any where, and at any time.

I have nothing of Vives, or Budaeus, and little of Erasmus. If the familiar histories of the saints, the want of which they regret, would have given us the histories of those tricks, which these writers acknolege to have been practiced, and of the lies they agree have been invented for the sake of religion, I join them in their regrets. These would be the only parts of their histories worth reading. It is not only the sacred volumes they have thus interpolated, gutted, and falsified, but the works of others relating to them, and even the laws of the land. We have a curious instance of one of those pious frauds in the Laws of Alfred. He composed, you know, from the laws of the Heptarchy, a Digest for the government of the United kingdom, and in his preface to that work he tells us expressly the sources from which he drew it, to wit, the laws of Ina. of Offa and Aethelbert, (not naming the pentateuch). But his pious Interpolator, very awkwardly, premises to his work four chapters of Exodus (from the 20th. to the 23rd.) as part of the laws of the land; so that Alfred's preface is made to stand in the body of the work. Our judges too have lent a ready hand to further these frauds, and have been willing to lay the yoke of their own opinions on the necks of others; to extend the coercions of municipal law to the dogmas of their religion, by declaring that these make a part of the law of the land. In the Year Book 34. H. 6, fo. 38. in Quare impedit [wherefore it obstructs], where the question was how far the common law takes notice of the Ecclesiastical law, Prisot, Chief Justice, in the course of his argument says *"tiels leis que ils de Seint eglise on en ancien scripture, covient a nous a donner credence; car ces*

Common ley sur quels touts manners leis sont fondes: et auxy, Sir, nous sumus obliges de conustre lour ley de saint eglise Etc." [To such laws of the church as have warrant in ancient writing our law giveth credence; for it is the common law on which all laws are based; and also, Sir, we are obliged to recognize the law of the church, etc.] Finch begins the business of falsification by mistranslating and misstating the words of Prisot thus "to such laws of the church as have warrant in holy scripture our law giveth credence," citing the above case and the words of Prisot in the margin Finch's law. B. I. c. 3. Here then we find ancien scripture, antient writing, translated "holy scripture." This, Wingate in 1658. erects into a Maxim of law, in the very words of Finch, but citing Prisot, and not Finch. And Sheppard tit. Religion, in 1675 laying it down in the same words as Finch, quotes the Year Book, Finch and Wingate. Then comes Sir Matthew Hale, in the case of the King vs. Taylor I Ventr. 293. e Keb. 607. and declares that "Christianity is parcel of the laws of England." Citing nobody, and resting it, with his judgment against the witches on his own authority, which indeed was sound and good in all cases into which no superstition or bigotry could enter. Thus strengthened, the court in 1728 in the King v. Wooston, would not suffer it to be questioned whether to write against Christianity was punishable at Common law, saying it had been settled by Hale in Taylor's case. 2 Stra. 834. Wood therefore, 409. without scruple, lays down as a principle that all blasphemy and profaneness are offences at the Common law, and cites Strange. Blackstone, in 1763. repeats in the words of Sr. Matthew Hale that "Christianity is part of the laws of England," citing Ventris and Strange *ubi supra* [as above]. And Ld. Mansfield in the case of the Chamberlain of London v. Evans, in 1767. qualifying somewhat the position, says that "the essential principles of revealed religion are part of the Common law." Thus we find this string of authorities all hanging by one another on a single hook, a mistranslation by Finch of the words of Prisot, or on nothing. For all quote Prisot, or one another, or nobody. Thus Finch misquotes Prisot;

Wingate also, but using Finch's words; Woolston's case cite Hale; Wood cites Woolston's case; Blackstone that and Hale; and Ld. Mansfield volunteers in his own *ipse dixit* [he himself has spoken]. And who now can question but that the whole Bible and Testament are a part of the Common law? And that Connecticut, in her blue laws, laying it down as a principle that the laws of god should be the laws of their land, except where their own contradicted them, did anything more than express, with a salvo, what the English judges had less cautiously declared without any restriction? And I dare say our cunning Chief Justice [John Marshall] would swear to, and find as many sophisms to twist it out of the general terms of our Declaration of rights, and even the stricter text of the Virginia "act for the freedom of religion" as he did to twist Burr's neck out of the halter for treason. May we not say then with him who was all candor and benevolence, "Woe unto you, ye lawyers, for ye lade men with burdens grievous to bear."

2. EXCERPT FROM A LETTER FROM THOMAS JEFFERSON TO MAJOR JOHN CARTWRIGHT, JUNE 5, 1824:

I was glad to find in your book a formal contradiction, at length, of the judiciary usurpation of legislative powers; for such the judges have usurped in their repeated decisions, that Christianity is a part of the common law. The proof of the contrary, which you have adduced, is incontrovertible; to wit, that the common law existed while the Anglo-Saxons were yet Pagans, at a time when they had never yet heard the name of Christ pronounced, or knew that such a character had ever existed. But it may amuse you, to shew when, and by what means, they stole this law in upon us. In a case of *quare impedit* [wherefore it obstructs] in the Year-book 34. H. 6. folio 38. (anno 1458,) a question was made, how far the ecclesiastical law was to be respected in a common law court? And Prisot, Chief Justice, gives his opinion in these words,

"A tiel leis qu'ils de seint eglise ont en ancien scripture, covient a nous a donner credence; car ceo common ley sur quels touts manners leis sont fondes. Et auxy, Sir, nous sumus obleges de conustre lour ley de saint eglise; et semblablement ils sont obliges de conustre nostre ley. Et, Sir, si poit apperer or a nous que l'evesque ad fait come un ordinary fera en tiel cas, adong nous devons ceo adjuger bon, ou auterment nemy."

["to such laws as those of holy church have in antient writing, it is proper for us to give credence; for the law is common as regards all affairs for which laws were founded. And, moreover, Sir, we are obliged to follow their laws regards the holy church: and in like manner they are obliged to follow our law. And, Sir, should it seem to us that the bishop acted as a layman in such a case, we should do well to deem him a common man, as much as not."] &c. See S.C. Fitzh. Abr. Qu. Imp. 89. Bro. Abr. Qu. Imp. 12. Finch in his first book, c. 3. is the first afterwards who quotes this case, and mistakes it thus. "To such laws of the church as have warrant in holy scripture, our law giveth credence." And cites Prisot; mistranslating "ancien scripture," into "holy scripture." Whereas Prisot palpably says, "to such laws as those of holy church have in antient writing, it is proper for us to give credence," to wit, to their antient written laws. This was in 1613, a century and a half after the dictum of Prisot. Wingate, in 1658, erects this false translation into a maxim of the common law, copying the words of Finch, but citing Prisot. Wing. Max. 3. And Sheppard, title, "Religion," in 1675, copies the same mistranslation, quoting the Y.B. Finch and Wingate. Hale expressess it in these words; "Christianity is parcel of the laws of England." 1 Ventr. 293. 3. Keb. 607. But he quotes no authority. By these echoings and re-echoings from one to another, it had become so established in 1728, that in the case of the King vs. Woolston, 2. Stra. 834, the court would not suffer it to be debated, whether to write against Christianity was punishable in the temporal court at common law? Wood, therefore, 409, ventures still

to vary the phrase, and say, that all blasphemy and profaneness are offences by the common law; and cites 2 Stra. Then Blackstone, in
1763, IV. 59, repeats the words of Hale, that "Christianity is part of
the laws of England," citing Ventris and Strange. And finally, Lord
Mansfield, with a little qualification, in Evans's case, in 1767, says,
that "the essential principles of revealed religion are part of the common law." Thus ingulphing Bible, Testament and all into the common law, without citing any authority. And thus we find this chain of
authorities hanging link by link, one upon another, and all ultimately
on one and the same hook, and that a mistranslation of the words "an
cien scripture," used by Prisot. Finch quotes Prisot; Wingate does the
same. Sheppard quotes Prisot, Finch and Wingate. Hale cites nobody. The court in Woolston's case, cites Hale. Wood cites Woolston's
case. Blackstone quotes Woolston's case and Hale. And Lord Mansfield, like Hale, ventures it on his own authority. Here I might defy
the best read lawyer to produce another scrip of authority for this judiciary forgery; and I might go on further to shew, how some of the
Anglo-Saxon priests interpolated into the text of Alfred's laws, the
20th, 21st, 22nd and 23rd chapters of Exodus, and the 15th of the Acts
of the Apostles, from the 23rd to the 29th verses. But this would lead
my pen and your patience too far. What a conspiracy this, between
Church and State! Sing Tantarara, rogues all, rogues all, Sing Tantarara, rogues all! . . .

Madison's "Memorial and Remonstrance Against Religious Assessments"

TO THE HONORABLE GENERAL ASSEMBLY OF THE COMMON-
WEALTH OF VIRGINIA: A MEMORIAL AND REMONSTRANCE

We, the subscribers, citizens of the said Commonwealth, having taken into serious consideration, a Bill printed by order of the last Session of General Assembly, entitled "A Bill establishing a provision for Teachers of the Christian Religion," and conceiving that the same if finally armed with the sanctions of a law, will be a dangerous abuse of power, are bound as faithful members of a free State to remonstrate against it, and to declare the reason by which we are determined. We remonstrate against the said Bill,

1. Because we hold it for a fundamental and undeniable truth, "that religion or the duty which we owe to our Creator and the manner of discharging it, can be directed only by reason and conviction, not by force or violence." The Religion then of every man must be left to the conviction and conscience of every man; and it is the right of

every man to exercise it as these may dictate. This right is in its nature an unalienable right. It is unalienable, because the opinions of men, depending only on the evidence contemplated by their own minds cannot follow the dictates of other men: It is unalienable also, because what is here a right towards men, is a duty towards the Creator. It is the duty of every man to render to the Creator such homage and such only as he believes to be acceptable to him. This duty is precedent, both in order of time and in degree of obligation, to the claims of Civil Society. Before any man can be considered as a member of Civil Society, he must be considered as a subject of the Governor of the Universe: And if a member of Civil Society, do it with a saving of his allegiance to the Universal Sovereign.

We maintain therefore that in matters of Religion, no man's right is abridged by the institution of Civil Society and that Religion is wholly exempt from its cognizance. True it is, that no other rule exists, by which any question which may divide a Society, can be ultimately determined, but the will of the majority; but it is also true that the majority may trespass on the rights of the minority.

2. Because Religion be exempt from the authority of the Society at large, still less can it be subject to that of the Legislative Body. The latter are but the creatures and viceregents of the former. Their jurisdiction is both derivative and limited: it is limited with regard to the coordinate departments, more necessarily it is limited with regard to the constituents. The preservation of a free Government requires not merely, that the metes and bounds which separate each department of power be invariably maintained; but more especially that neither of them be suffered to overleap the great Barrier which defends the rights of the people. The Rulers who are guilty of such an encroachment, exceed the commission from which they derive their authority, and are Tyrants. The People who submit to it are governed by laws made neither by themselves nor by an authority derived from them, and are slaves.

3. Because it is proper to take alarm at the first experiment on our liberties. We hold this prudent jealousy to be the first duty of Citizens, and one of the noblest characteristics of the late Revolution. The free men of America did not wait till usurped power had strengthened itself by exercise, and entangled the question in precedents. They saw all the consequences in the principle, and they avoided the consequences by denying the principle. We revere this lesson too much soon to forget it. Who does not see that the same authority which can establish Christianity, in exclusion of all other Religions, may establish with the same ease any particular sect of Christians, in exclusion of all other Sects? that the same authority which can force a citizen to contribute three pence only of his property for the support of any one establishment, may force him to conform to any other establishment in all cases whatsoever?

4. Because the Bill violates the equality which ought to be the basis of every law, and which is more indispensible, in proportion as the validity or expediency of any law is more liable to be impeached. If "all men are by nature equally free and independent," all men are to be considered as entering into Society on equal conditions; as relinquishing no more, and therefore retaining no less, one than another, of their natural rights. Above all are they to be considered as retaining an "*equal* title to the free exercise of Religion according to the dictates of Conscience." Whilst we assert for ourselves a freedom to embrace, to profess and to observe the Religion which we believe to be of divine origin, we cannot deny an equal freedom to those whose minds have not yet yielded to the evidence which has convinced us. If this freedom be abused, it is an offence against God, not against man: To God, therefore, not to man, must an account of it be rendered. As the Bill violates equality by subjecting some to peculiar burdens, so it violates the same principle, by granting to others peculiar exemptions. Are the Quakers and Menonists the only sects who think a compulsive support of their Religions unnecessary and

unwarrantable? Can their piety alone be entrusted with the care of public worship? Ought their Religions to be endowed above all others with extraordinary privileges by which proselytes may be enticed from all others? We think too favorably of the justice and good sense of these denominations to believe that they either covet pre-eminece over their fellow citizens or that they will be seduced by them from the common opposition to the measure.

5. Because the Bill implies either that the Civil Magistrate is a competent Judge of Religious Truth; or that he may employ Religion as an engine of Civil policy. The first is an arrogant pretension falsified by the contradictory opinions of all Rulers in all ages, and throughout the world: the second an unhallowed perversion of the means of salvation.

6. Because the establishment proposed by the Bill is not requisite for the support of the Christian Religion itself, for every page of it disavows a dependence on the powers of this world: it is a contradiction to fact; for it is known that this Religion both existed and flourished, not only without the support of human laws, but in spite of every opposition from them, and not only during the period of miraculous aid, but long after it had been left to its own evidence and the ordinary care of Providence. Nay, it is a contradiction in terms; for a Religion not invented by human policy, must have pre-existed and been supported, before it was established by human policy. It is moreover to awaken in those who profess this Religion by a pious confidence in its innate excellence and the patronage of its Author; and to foster in those who still reject it, a suspicion that its friends are too conscious of its fallacies to trust it to its own merits.

7. Because experience witnisseth that ecclesiastical establishments, instead of maintaining the purity and efficacy of Religion, have had a contrary operation. During almost fifteen centuries has the legal establishment of Christianity been on trial. What have been its fruits? More or less in all places, pride and indolence in the Clergy,

ignorance and servility in the laity, in both, superstition, bigotry and persecution. Enquire of the Teachers of Christianity for the ages in which it appeared in its greatest lustre; those of every sect, point to the ages prior to its incorporation with Civil policy. Propose a restoration of this primitive State in which its Teachers depended on the voluntary rewards of their flocks, many of them predict its downfall. On which Side ought their testimony to have the greatest weight, when for or when against their interest?

8. Because the establishment in question is not necessary for the support of Civil Government. If it be urged as necessary for the support of Civil Government only as it is a means of supporting Religion, and it be not necessary for the latter purpose, it cannot be necessary for the former. If Religion be not within the cognizance of the Civil Government how can its legal establishment be necessary to Civil Government? What influence in fact have ecclesiastical establishments had on Civil Society? In some instances they have been seen to erect a spiritual tyranny on the ruins of the Civil authority; in many instances they have been seen upholding the thrones of political tyranny; in no instance have they been seen as the guardians of the liberties of the people. Rulers who wished to subvert the public liberty, may have found an established Clergy convenient auxiliaries. A just Government instituted to secure & perpetuate it needs them not. Such a Government will be best supported by protecting every Citizen in the enjoyment of his Religion with the same equal hand which protects his person and his property; by neither invading the equal rights of any Sect, nor suffering any Sect to invade those of another.

9. Because the propsed establishment is a departure from that generous policy, which, offering an Asylum to the persecuted and oppressed of every Nation and Religion, promised a lustre to our country, and an accession to the number of its citizens. What a melancholy mark is the Bill of sudden degeneracy? Instead of holding forth an Asylum to the persecuted, it is itself a signal of persecution. It degrades from the

equal rank of Citizens all those whose opinions in Religion do not bend to those of the Legislative authority. Distant as it may be in its present form from the Inquisition, it differs from it only in degree. The one is the first step, the other the last in the career of intolerance. The magnanimous sufferer under this cruel scourge in foreign Regions, must view the Bill as a Beacon on our Coast, warning him to seek some other haven, where liberty and philanthropy in their due extent, may offer a more certain repose from his Troubles.

10. Because it will have a like tendency to banish our Citizens. The allurements presented by other situations are every day thinning their number. To superadd a fresh motive to emigration by revoking the liberty which they now enjoy, would be the same species of folly which has dishonoured and depopulated flourishing kingdoms.

11. Because it will destroy that moderation and harmony which the forbearance of our laws to intermeddle with Religion has produced among its several sects. Torrents of blood have been spilt in the old world, by vain attempts of the secular arm, to extinguish Religious discord, by proscribing all difference in Religious opinion. Time has at length revealed the true remedy. Every relaxation of narrow and rigorous policy, wherever it has been tried, has been found to assuage the disease. The American Theatre has exhibited proofs that equal and compleat liberty, if it does not wholly eradicate it, sufficiently destroys its malignant influence on the health and prosperity of the State. If with the salutary effects of this system under our own eyes, we begin to contract the bounds of Religious freedom, we know no name that will too severely reproach our folly. At least let warning be taken at the first fruits of the threatened innovation. The very appearance of the Bill has transformed "that Christian forbearance, love and charity," which of late mutually prevailed, into animosities and jealousies, which may not soon be appeased. What mischiefs may not be dreaded, should this enemy to the public quiet be armed with the force of a law?

12. Because the policy of the Bill is adverse to the diffusion of the light of Christianity. The first wish of those who enjoy this precious gift ought to be that it may be imparted to the whole race of mankind. Compare the number of those who have as yet received it with the number still remaining under the dominion of false Religions; and how small is the former! Does the policy of the Bill tend to lessen the disproportion? No; it at once discourges those who are strangers to the light of revelation from coming into the Region of it; and countenaces by example the nations who continue in darkness, in shutting out those who might convey it to them. Instead of Levelling as far as possible, every obstacle to the victorious progress of Truth, the Bill with an ignoble and unchristian timidity would circumscribe it with a wall of defence against the encroachments of error.

13. Because attempts to enforce by legal sanctions, acts obnoxious to so great a proportion of Citizens, tend to enervate the laws in general, and to slacken the bands of Society. If it be difficult to execute any law which is not generally deemed necessary or salutary, what must be the case, where it is deemed invalid and dangerous? And what may be the effect of so striking an example of impotency in the Government, on its general authority?

14. Because a measure of such singular magnitude and delicacy ought not to be imposed, without the clearest evidence that it is called for by a majority of citizens, and no satisfactory method is yet proposed by which the voice of the majority in this case may be determined, or its influence secured. "The people of the respective counties are indeed requested to signify their opinion respecting the adoption of the Bill to the next Session of Assembly." But the representation must be made equal, before the voice either of the Representatives or of the Counties will be that of the people. Our hope is that neither of the former will, after due consideration, espouse the dangerous principle of the Bill. Should the event disappoint us, it

will still leave us in full confidence, that a fair appeal to the latter will reverse the sentence against our liberties.

15. Because finally, "the equal right of every citizen to the free exercise of his Religion according to the dictates of conscience" is held by the same tenure with all our other rights. If we recur to its origin, it is equally the gift of nature; if we weight its importance, it cannot be less dear to us; if we consult the "Declaration of those rights which pertain to the good people of Virginia, as the basis and foundation of Government," it is enumerated with equal solemnity, or rather studied emphasis. Either then, we must say, that the Will of the Legislature is the only measure of their authority; and that in the plenitude of this authority, they may sweep away all our fundamental rights; or, that they are bound to leave this particular right untouched and sacred: Either we must say, that they may controul the freedom of the press, may abolish the Trial by Jury, may swallow up the executive and Judiciary Powers of the State; nay that they may despoil us of our very right of suffrage, and erect themselves into an independent and hereditary Assembly or, we must say, that they have no authority to enact into law the Bill under consideration. We the Subscribers say, that the General Assembly of this Commonwealth have no such authority: And that no effort may be omitted on our part against so dangerous an usurpation, we oppose to it, this remonstrance; earnestly praying, as we are in duty bound, that the Supreme Lawgiver of the Universe, by illuminating those to whom it is addressed, may on the one hand, turn their Councils from every act which would affront his holy prerogative, or violate the trust committed to them: and on the other, guide them into every measure which may be worthy of his [blessing, may re]dound to their own praise, and may establish more firmly the liberties, the prosperity and the happiness of the Commonwealth.

Notes

PREFACE

page

xii "We forgot . . .": Ron Chernow, *Alexander Hamilton: A Life* (New York, 2004), 235.

xii "in four short Words . . .": John Adams to Thomas Jefferson, December 12, 1816, in *The Adams-Jefferson Letters: The Complete Correspondence Between Thomas Jefferson and John Adams*, ed. Lester J. Cappon (Chapel Hill, 1987; first published 1959), 499.

xiii "Religious bondage shackles . . .": James Madison to William Bradford, April 1, 1774, in *James Madison: Writings*, ed. Jack N. Rakove (New York, 1999), 9.

xiii–xiv "Our Western institutions . . .": Louis Dupré, *The Enlightenment and the Intellectual Traditions of Modern Culture* (New Haven, 2004), 153.

CHAPTER ONE: FRANKLIN

3 "snatched lightning from the sky . . .": Walter Isaacson, *Benjamin Franklin: An American Life* (New York, 2003), 145.

3 "the new Prometheus . . .": *ibid.*

3 "first philosopher," "first great man of letters . . .": David Hume to Franklin, May 10, 1762, *ibid.*, 197.

3–4 "There presently arose a general cry . . .": *The Portable John Adams*, ed. John Patrick Diggins (New York, 2004), 69.

4 "our free-thinkers . . .": Isaacson, 371.

4–5 "'All religions are tolerated in America . . .'": Diggins, 97.

5 "I oppose *my theist* . . .": Benjamin Franklin to [Thomas Hopkinson?], October 16, 1746, in Leonard W. Labaree, *Papers of Benjamin Franklin* (New Haven, 1961), III, 88.

5 "observations of Quakers . . .": Henry F. May, *The Enlightenment in America* (New York, 1976), 127.

6 "This obscure family of ours . . .": *Autobiography. A Benjamin Franklin Reader*, ed. Nathan G. Goodman (New York, 1971), 50.

7 "My mother . . . was Abiah Folger . . .": *ibid.*, 51.

7–8 "My father, in the meantime . . .": *ibid.*, 52.

8 "the Calvinism in which he was bred . . .": Vernon Louis Parrington, *Main Currents in American Thought, I: The Colonial Mind* (New York, 1927), 165.

8 "My father's little library . . .": *Autobiography*, 55.

8 "of Dr. Mather's . . .": *ibid.*

8 "a real doubter . . .": *ibid.*, 59.

9 "My parents had early given me . . .": *ibid.*, 96.

9 "my indiscreet disputations . . .": *ibid.*, 63.

9 "from the attributes of God . . .": *ibid.*, 96.

9 "I began to suspect . . .": *ibid.*

9–10 "Revelation had indeed no weight with me . . .": *ibid.*, 97.

10 "*truth, sincerity* and *integrity* . . .": *ibid.*

10 "I had been religiously educated . . .": *ibid.*, 117–118.

11 "A loaf of sugar . . .": cited in Carl van Doren, *Benjamin Franklin* (New York, 1938), 645.

11 "My mother grieves . . .": Franklin to Josiah Franklin, April 13, 1778, in *Autobiography*, 232.

11-12 "The faith you mention . . .": Franklin to Joseph Huey, June 6, 1753; *ibid.*, 235.

12 "When I traveled in Flanders . . .": Franklin to Jared Ingersoll, December 11, 1762, in Labaree, X, 175–176.

12–13 "Tho' I seldom attended . . .": *Autobiography*, 118.

13 "A man of Words . . .": Franklin to Jane Mecom, October 16, 1758, in Labaree, VIII, 155.

14 "our particular superstition . . .": Jefferson to William Short, April 13, 1820, in Lenni Brenner, ed., *Jefferson and Madison on Separation of Church and State: Writings on Religion and Secularism* (Fort Lee, N.J., 2004), 336.

14 "If we look back into history . . .": Letter to the *London Packet*, June 3, 1772, in Labaree, XIX, 164.

14 "most sects in religion . . .": From a speech delivered during the Constitutional Convention. Franklin, *"The Autobiography" and Other Writings on Politics, Economics, and Virtue*, ed. Alan Houston (Cambridge, England, 2004), 332.

14 "This modesty in a sect . . .": *Autobiography*, 150–151.

15–16 "A Swedish minister . . .": "Remarks Concerning the Savages of North America," in Houston, 332.

16 "A disputatious turn . . .": *Autobiography*, 56–57.

16 "I was charmed with it . . .": *ibid.*, 59–60.

17 "[T]hough your reasonings are subtile . . .": Franklin [to Thomas Paine], July 3, 1786, cited in H. W. Brands, *The First American: The Life and Times of Benjamin Franklin* (New York, 2000), 658.

17 "It has been for some Time . . .": Franklin writing as "Silence Dogood," *New England Courant*, July 23, 1722.

18 "a vicious man . . .": *Pennsylvania Gazette*, June 23, 1730.

18 "virtue was not secure . . .": *Pennsylvania Gazette*, July 9, 1730.

18 "Both before and after . . .": A. O. Aldridge, *Benjamin Franklin: Philosopher and Man* (Philadelphia, 1965), 53.

19 "His eloquence . . .": *Autobiography*, 141.

19 "I happened soon after . . .": *ibid.*

19–20 "He had a loud and clear voice . . .": *ibid.*, 142–143.

21 "I do not despair . . .": George Whitefield to Franklin, November 23, 1740, in Labaree, II, 270.

21 "[A]s you have made . . .": Whitefield to Franklin, August 17, 1752, *ibid.*, IV, 343.

21 "u'sd, indeed, sometimes . . .": *Autobiography*, 142.

21 "He reply'd . . .": *ibid.*

22 "It is much to be lamented . . .": Joseph Priestley, *Autobiography* (Teaneck, N.J., 1970), 117.

22 "not so much to secure religion . . .": Franklin to Richard Price, October 9, 1780, in Labaree, XXXIII, 390.

22–23 "I agreed with you . . .": John E. Remsberg, *Six Historic Americans*, 1906, chapter 4. Available on www.infidels.org/library/historical

23 "as to confer . . .": Benjamin Rush to Richard Price, April 22, 1786, in L. H. Butterfield, ed., *Letters of Benjamin Rush* (Princeton, 1951), I, 385–386.

23 "The Convention . . .": in van Doren, 748.

24 "Here is my creed . . .": Franklin to Ezra Stiles, March 9, 1790, in *Autobiography*, 244.

25 "I confide . . ." *ibid.*, 245.

CHAPTER TWO: WASHINGTON

26–27 "Doctor [Benjamin] Rush tells me . . .": Jefferson, *Anas*, February 4, 1818, cited in Brenner, 266–267.

27 "upon the subject . . .": Rush to Adams, December 15, 1807, in John A. Schultz and Douglass Adair, eds., *The Spur of Fame: Dialogues of John Adams and Benjamin Rush, 1805–1813* (Indianapolis, 2001), 108.

27 "Washington! Franklin! . . .": Adams to Rush, July 23, 1806, *ibid.*, 64.

27 "knew no man who seemed . . .": Reverend Bird Wilson, D.D., *Memoir of the Life of the Right Reverend William White, D.D.* (Philadelphia, 1839), 190.

27 "unusual but uniform . . .": cited in Peter R. Henriques, "George Washington and Religion: A Talk for the Teachers Institute at Mount Vernon," July 21, 1999.

28 "a lukewarm Episcopalian . . .": Joseph J. Ellis, *His Excellency: George Washington* (New York, 2004), 45.

29 "more as an instrument . . .": Frank Lambert, *The Founding Fathers and the Place of Religion in America* (Princeton, 2003), 72.

29 "a local oligarchy . . .": H. J. Eckenrode, *Separation of Church and State in Virginia* (Richmond, 1912), 13.

29 "It is hardly possible . . .": Washington to William Pearce, January 17, 1796; January 31, 1796, in *George Washington Bicentennial Edition: The Papers of George Washington* (Washington, D.C., 1931), XXXIV, 423.

29–30 "It is not convenient . . .": Washington to Daniel McCarty, February 22, 1784, *ibid.*, XXVII, 341.

30 "No one can pretend . . .": Louis B. Wright, *The First Gentlemen of Virginia* (San Marino, Calif., 1940), 66–67.

30 "[Planter] society seemed . . .": May, 68.

31 "The stories of Washington's piety . . .": 1846 interview with Ona Judge Staines. Cited in "Letter to the Editor" by the Reverend Benjamin Chase in *The Liberator*, January 1, 1947.

31 "The first time that I dined with him . . .": cited in Franklin Steiner, *The Religious Beliefs of Our Presidents* (Amherst, N.Y., 1995; first published 1936), 23.

32 "I have a desire . . .": cited in Wilson, *Memoir*, 196–197.

32 "Dear Sir . . .": *ibid.*, 197.

32–33 "One incident . . .": Reverend William B. Sprague, D.D., *Annals of the American Pulpit* (New York, 1859), V, 394.

33 "there were no ministers in the room . . .": Ellis, 269.

33–34 "the inevitable renderings . . .": *ibid.*

34 "His behavior [in church] . . .": Wilson, *Memoir*, 189.

34 "Although I was often in company . . .": *ibid.*, 190.

34 "I do not believe . . .": *ibid.*, 193.

34 "was esteemed by the whole world . . .": Reverend Bird Wilson, D.D., Sermon, *Albany Daily Advertiser*, cited in Paul F. Boller, *George Washington and Religion* (Dallas, 1963), 14–15.

34 "Sir, Washington was a Deist . . .": cited in Steiner, 26–27.

35 "the effort to depict Washington . . .": A. W. Greely, "Washington's Domestic and Religious Life," *Ladies Home Journal*, April 1896.

35 "in several thousand letters . . .": *ibid.*

36 "The determinations of Providence . . .": Washington to Bryan Fairfax, March 1, 1778, in *Bicentennial Edition*, XI, 3.

36 "In what way they will terminate . . .": cited in Henriques.

37 "The virtues of the [Virginia] gentleman . . .": Wright, 9.

37–38 "How to act . . .": Marcus Aurelius, *Meditations*, translated and with an introduction by Gregory Hays (New York, 2003), 30.

38–39 "I have sometimes . . .": Adams to Rush, September 1807, in Schutz and Adair, 102–103.

40 "few and simple . . .": Edwin S. Gaustad, "Disciples of Reason," *Christian History*, Spring 1996.

40 "no bigot to any form of worship . . .": Washington to the Marquis de Lafayette, August 15, 1787, in *Bicentennial Edition*, XXIX, 259.

40 "While men perform . . .": letter to the annual meeting of Quakers, September 28, 1789, *ibid.*, XXX, 416 n.

40 "We have abundant reason . . .": January 27, 1793, *ibid.*, XXXII, 315.

40 "The Citizens of the United States . . .": August 18, 1790, *ibid.*, XXXI, 93 n. More fully in John Rhodehamel, ed., *George Washington: Writings* (New York, 1997), 767.

41 "As mankind becomes more liberal . . .": March 15, 1790, in *Bicentennial Edition*, XXXI, 22.

41 "Government being . . .": September 28, 1789, *ibid.*, XXX, 416 n.

41 "I am persuaded . . .": October 28, 1789, *ibid.*, XXX, 453.

41 "I now send . . .": August 29, 1796, *ibid.*, XXXV, 198.

41–42 "If we did a good act . . .": Jefferson to Thomas Law, June 13, 1814, in Merrill D. Peterson, ed., *Thomas Jefferson: Writings* (New York, 1984), 1336.

42 "The Commander in chief . . .": March 22, 1783, in *Bicentennial Edition*, XXVI, 250.

42 "there exists . . .": *First Inaugural Address*, Rhodehamel 732–733.

43 "I've something to whisper . . .": Mason L. Weems, *The Life of Washington*, with an introduction by Marcus Cunliffe (Cambridge, Mass., 1962), xv.

43–44 "American nationalism . . .": *ibid.*, xliii.

45 "When the children . . .": *ibid.*, 172.

45–46 "In the winter of '77 . . .": *ibid.*, 181–182.

46–47 "Feeling that the hour . . .": *ibid.*, 168.

47 "idolatrous worship . . .": Rush to Adams, July 8, 1812, in Schutz and Adair, 250.

47 "the impious application . . .": *ibid.*

47 "Owing to the pernicious drivel . . .": William Roscoe Thayer, *George Washington* (Boston, 1922), vii.

CHAPTER THREE: ADAMS

49 "I mix religion . . .": Adams to Rush, April 12, 1809, in Schutz and Adair, 155.

49 "I must be . . .": Adams to the Reverend Samuel Miller, July 7, 1820, in James H. Huston, *The Founders on Religion: A Book of Quotations* (Princeton, 2005), 38.

50 "All sober inquirers . . .": *Thoughts on Government*, in Diggins, 234.

50–51 "[T]he nature of mankind . . .": Diggins, xxv–xxvi.

51 "The Loss of Paradise . . .": Adams to Jefferson, October 9, 1787, in Cappon, 202.

52 "a Spirit of Dogmatism . . .": L. H. Butterfield, ed., *Diary and Autobiography of John Adams* (Cambridge, Mass., Adams Papers, 1962), III, 262.

52 "*Rights,* that cannot be repealed . . .": *Dissertation of Canon and Feudal Law,* in Diggins, 210–211.

53 "This day I went . . .": Adams to Abigail Adams, October 9, 1774, in Frank Shuffelton, ed., *Letters of John and Abigail Adams* (New York, 2004), 43.

53–54 "This afternoon . . .": *ibid.*, 43–44.

54–55 "When the Congress first met . . .": Adams to Abigail Adams, September 16, 1774, *ibid.*, 34–35.

55 "for the Support . . .": Adams to Abigail Adams, October 29, 1775, *ibid.*, 119.

56 "a change in the solar system . . .": cited in Morton Borden, *Jews, Turks and Infidels* (Chapel Hill, 1984), 12.

49 "a man of learning and ingenuity . . . to be good politicians . . .": Adams to
56 Adams, September 17, 1775, in Shuffleton, 97.

56 "Aristocratical tyrants . . .": Adams to Rush, December 27, 1810, in Schutz and Adair, 189.

57 "Ask me not, then . . .": Adams to Rush, January 21, 1810, *ibid.*, 175.

57 "For more than sixty years . . .": Adams to Jefferson, July 18, 1813, in Cappon, 361.

57–58 "For the last Year or two . . .": Adams to Jefferson, December 12, 1816, *ibid.*, 499.

58 "Philosophy is not only . . .": Adams to Jefferson, December 25, 1813, *ibid.*, 412.

58 "a church-going animal . . .": Adams to Abigail Adams, January 28, 1799, cited in John Ferling, *John Adams: A Life* (New York, 1992), 433.

58 "Honour the Gods . . . of this rule . . .": Adams to Jefferson, December 3, 1813, in Cappon, 402.

59 "The human Understanding . . .": Adams to Jefferson, September 14, 1813, *ibid.*, 373.

60 "I labored through the tedious toil . . .": Adams to Jefferson, July 16, 1814, *ibid.*, 437.

60 "It may be thought impiety . . .": Adams to Jefferson, May 3, 1812, *ibid.*, 302.

61 "Perhaps we may laugh . . .": Adams to Jefferson, May 29, 1818, *ibid.*, 526.

62 "I wish you, Mr. Madison and Mr. Monroe . . .": Adams to Jefferson, May 18, 1817, *ibid.*, 516.

62 "I leave those profound Phylosophers . . .": Adams to Jefferson, February 2, 1816, *ibid.*, 462.

62 "*Bos, fur, sus* . . .": Adams to Rush, July 10, 1812, in Schutz and Adair, 251.

62 "Oh! Lord! . . .": Adams to Jefferson, May 18, 1817, in Cappon, 515.

62–63 "[T]here is a germ of religion . . .": Adams to Rush, June 12, 1812, in Schutz and Adair, 244.

63 "The multitude and diversity of them . . .": Adams to Jefferson, May 18, 1817, in Cappon, 515.

63–64 "Religious Controversies . . .": Adams to Jefferson, February [–March 3] 1814, *ibid.*, 427.

64 "turned me out of office . . . a century to come . . .": Adams to Rush, June 12, 1812, in Schutz and Adair, 244.

65 "I cannot contemplate human Affairs . . .": Adams to Jefferson, July 15, 1817, in Cappon, 519.

65–66 "We think ourselves possessed . . .": Adams to Jefferson, January 23, 1825, *ibid.*, 607–608.

66 "Instead of the most enlightened . . .": Adams to Rush, December 28, 1807, in Schutz and Adair, 110.

67 "[A]ccording to the few lights . . .": Adams to Jefferson, November 13, 1815, in Cappon, 456.

67–68 "I am weary . . .": Adams to Jefferson, June 28, 1812, *ibid.*, 310.

68 "That there is an active principle . . .": Adams to Jefferson, January 22, 1825, *ibid.*, 607.

68 "if we are disappointed . . .": Adams to Jefferson, February 25, 1825, *ibid.*, 610.

68 "I am certainly very near . . .": Adams to Jefferson, January 14, 1826, *ibid.*, 613.

69 "This world is a mixture . . .": Adams to Jefferson, September 15, 1813, *ibid.*, 376.

CHAPTER FOUR: JEFFERSON

70 "History, I believe . . .": Jefferson to Alexander von Humboldt, December 6, 1813, in Peterson, 1311.

71 "The error seems . . .": *Notes on the State of Virginia: The Life and Selected Writings of Thomas Jefferson*, eds. Adrienne Koch and William Peden (New York, 2004; first published 1944), 254–255.

71 "Let my neighbor . . .": Reverend William Linn, *Serious Considerations on the Election of a President: Addressed to the Citizens of the United States* (New York, 1800), article 19.

72 "our particular superstition . . .": Jefferson to William Short, April 13, 1820, in Brenner, 336.

72 "a being of terrific character . . .": Jefferson to William Short, August 4, 1820, in Peterson, 1437.

72 "In every country . . .": Jefferson to Horatio Gates Spofford, March 17, 1814, in Brenner, 224.

72 "a fabulous polymath . . .": Bernard Bailyn, *To Begin the World Anew* (New York, 2004), 41.

72–73 "Believing with you . . .": Jefferson to the Committee of the Danbury Baptist Association, January 1, 1802, in Peterson, 510.

73 "the *genus irritabile vatum* . . . in their position . . .": Jefferson to Rush, September 23, 1800, *ibid.*, 1082.

75 "the only oracle given you by heaven . . .": Jefferson to Peter Carr, August 10, 1787, *ibid.*, 904.

75 "religion retreats as philosophy advances . . .": Denis Diderot to Sophie Volland, October 30, 1759, *Correspondence* (Paris, 1955), eds. George Roth and Jean Varloot, 297.

75 "feared that spirit . . .": Marie-Jean-Antoine-Nicolas Caritat, Marquis de Condorcet: *Esquisse . . . Oeuvres*, eds. A. Condorcet O'Connor and M. F. Arago (1847), VI, 103.

75 "the three greatest men . . .": Jefferson to John Trumbull, February 15, 1789, in Peterson, 939–940.

75–77 "Religion. Your reason . . .": Jefferson to Peter Carr, August 10, 1787, *ibid.*, 902–903.

77–78 "It is between 50. And 60. Years . . .": Jefferson to Alexander Smyth, January 17, 1825, in Brenner, 385.

78 "artificial systems . . .": Jefferson to William Short, October 31, 1819, in Peterson, 1431.

78 "The immaculate conception of Jesus . . .": *ibid.*, 1431 n.

78 "The day will come . . .": Jefferson to Adams, April 11, 1823, in Cappon, 594.

79 "the hocus-pocus phantasm . . .": Jefferson to James Smith, December 8, 1822, in Brenner, 366.

79 "That Jesus did not mean . . .": Jefferson to William Short, August 4, 1820, in Peterson, 1437–1438.

79 "the most sublime . . .": Jefferson to Adams, October 12, 1813, in Cappon, 384.

80 "the metaphysical abstractions of Athanasius . . .": Jefferson to John Davis, January 18, 1824, in Brenner, 373.

80–81 "Every religion consists . . .": Jefferson to James Fishback, September 27, 1809, *ibid.*, 195.

81 "Of this band of dupes . . .": Jefferson to William Short, April 13, 1820, *ibid.*, 336.

81–82 "If we could believe . . .": Jefferson to William Short, August 4, 1820, in Peterson, 1435.

82 "low state," "wretched depravity . . .": Jefferson to Adams, October 12, 1813, in Cappon, 383–384.

82 "In extracting the pure principles . . . of Nonsense . . .": *ibid.*, 384.

82 "I have performed this operation . . .": *ibid.*

83 "I have read his Corruptions . . .": Jefferson to Adams, August 22, 1813, *ibid.*, 369.

83 "the assent of the mind . . .": *ibid.*, 368.

83–84 "The Christian priesthood . . .": Jefferson to Adams, July 5, 1814, *ibid.*, 433.

84 "constitutes the power . . .": Jefferson to Adams, August 22, 1813, *ibid.*, 368.

84 "the mountebanks calling themselves the priests of Jesus . . . a pursuing enemy.": Jefferson to Francis Van der Kemp, July 30, 1816, in Brennern, 248.

84 "dread the advance of science . . .": Jefferson to Francesco Correa da Serra, April 11, 1820, *ibid.*, 335.

84 "every priest who really understands . . .": H. L. Mencken, *Treatise on the Gods*, 2nd ed. (Baltimore, 1997), 27.

84–85 "The Presbyterian clergy . . .": Jefferson to William Short, April 13, 1820, in Brenner, 336.

85 "in the districts where Presbyterianism . . .": Jefferson to Dr. Thomas Cooper, November 2, 1822, in Peterson, 1464.

85 "light and liberality . . .": Jefferson to Adams, May 5, 1817, in Cappon, 512.

85 "this den of the priesthood . . .": *ibid.*

85 "whip and crop, pillory and roast . . .": Adams to Jefferson, May 18, 1817, *ibid.*, 515.

86 "I too am an Epicurian . . . of the Stoics . . .": Jefferson to William Short, October 31, 1819, in Peterson, 1430.

86 "that the human mind . . .": Jefferson to Adams, January 22, 1821, in Cappon, 569.

86 "instinct, and innate . . .": Jefferson to Adams, October 14, 1816, *ibid.*, 492.

86–87 "[N]ature hath implanted . . .": Jefferson to Thomas Law, June 13, 1814, in Peterson, 1337.

87 "If we did a good act . . .": *ibid.*, 1336.

87 "All persons shall have . . .": Brenner, 22–23.

87 "Our Saviour chose not . . .": *ibid.*, 27.

88 "The life & essence . . .": *ibid.*

88 "If any man err . . .": *ibid.*, 28.

88 "No man complains . . .": *ibid.*

88 "Locke denies toleration . . .": *ibid.*, 29–30.

88 "If magistracy should vouchsafe . . .": *ibid.*, 30.

89 "religious slavery . . .": *Notes on the State of Virginia*, Koch and Peden, 254.

89–90 "Reason and experiment . . .": *ibid.*, 255–256.

92–93 "was rejected by a great majority . . .": *Autobiography*, Koch and Peden, 46.

93 "with infinite approbation . . .": Jefferson to Madison, December 16, 1786, in James Morton Smith, ed., *The Republic of Letters: The Correspondence Between Jefferson and Madison, 1776–1826* (New York, 1995), 458.

93 "in fact it is comfortable . . .": *ibid.*

93–94 "Oh Lord . . .": G. Adolph Koch, *Republican Religion* (New York, 1933), 272.

94 "proceeded so far at last . . .": John Trumbull, *Autobiography* (New Haven, 1953), 170–171.

95 "THE GRAND QUESTION STATED . . .": *Gazette of the United States*, September 11 and 27, 1800; October 9, 1800.

95 "the great arch priest of Jacobinism and infidelity . . .": Theophilus Parsons to John Jay, May 5, 1800, in *The Correspondence and Public Papers of John Jay*, ed. Henry P. Johnston, 4 vols. (New York, 1893), IV, 270.

95 "Murder, robbery, rape . . .": James Roger Sharp, *American Politics in the Early Republic: The New Nation in Crisis* (New Haven, 1993), 227.

96 "With the Baptists . . .": Adams to Mercy Otis Warren, August 8, 1807, in Lambert, 281.

96 "When I was in Connecticut . . .": Thomas Paine to Jefferson, January 25, 1805, in Philip S. Foner, ed., *Complete Writings of Thomas Paine* (New York, 1945), II, 1460.

96–97 "I consider the government . . .": Jefferson to the Reverend Samuel Miller, January 23, 1808, in Peterson, 1186–1187.

97–98 "I am aware . . .": *ibid.*

98 "just well enough endowed . . .": Jefferson to Priestley, January 18, 1800, *ibid.*, 1070.

98 "The College of William and Mary . . .": *Autobiography*, Koch and Peden, 48.

98 "so broad and liberal . . .": Jefferson to Priestley, January 18, 1800, in Peterson, 1070.

99 "In conformity with . . .": Report of the Commissioners for the University of Virginia, in Brenner, 270–271.

99–100 "These reverend leaders . . .": Jefferson to Dr. Benjamin Waterhouse, October 13, 1815, *ibid.*, 237–238.

100 "In our Richmond . . .": Jefferson to Dr. Thomas Cooper, November 2, 1822, in Peterson, 1464.

100 "You judge truly . . .": Jefferson to Horation Gates Spofford, January 10, 1816, in Brenner, 240.

101 "For we know that the common law . . .": Jefferson to Dr. Thomas Cooper, February 10, 1814, in Peterson, 1325.

CHAPTER FIVE: MADISON

103 "There is not a shadow . . .": Madison, "General Defense of the Constitution, Virginia Ratification Convention," June 12, 1788, in Brenner, 96.

105 "Religious bondage shackles . . .": Madison to William Bradford, April 1, 1774, in Rakove, 9.

105 "Union of Religious Sentiments . . .": Madison to William Bradford, January 24, 1774, *ibid.*, 5–6.

105 "The finiteness of the human understanding . . .": Madison to Frederick Beasley, November 20, 1825, in Brenner, 388.

106 "inflamed [men and women] . . .": Madison, *Federalist* 10, in Rakove, 162.

106 "That as Religion . . .": George Mason, draft for *Virginia Declaration of Rights*, in Brenner, 21.

106–107 "That Religion or the duty . . .": Madison, proposed amendment to the *Virginia Declaration of Rights*, in Brenner, 21.

107 "During the session . . .": Madison to George Mason, Jr., July 14, 1826, in Brenner, 392.

108 ". . .Col. George Mason . . .": *ibid.*

108 "The Episcopal Clergy . . .": Madison to Jefferson, July 3, 1784, in Smith, I, 323.

108 "While Mr. Henry lives . . .": Jefferson to Madison, December 8, 1784, *ibid.*, 353–354.

109 "The opposition to the general assessment . . .": Madison to Jefferson, August 20, 1785, *ibid.*, 374.

109–110 "It gives me much pleasure . . .": Madison to James Monroe, May 29, 1785, in Brenner, 66.

110 "a dangerous abuse of power . . .": Preamble to *A Memorial and Remonstrance*; see Appendix II.

110 "[I]n matters of Religion . . .": Madison, *A Memorial and Remonstrance*, Article One.

110 "[I]t is proper . . .": *ibid.*, Article Three.

111 "unalienable . . .": *ibid.*, Article One.

111 "an offense against God . . .": *ibid.*, Article Four.

111 "What influence in fact . . .": *ibid.*, Article Four.

111 "During almost fifteen centuries . . .": *ibid.*, Article Seven.

111–112 "Because the Bill implies . . .": *ibid.*, Article Five.

112 "the number of Copies . . .": Madison, *Detached Memoranda*, in Brenner, 262.

112 "The enacting clauses . . .": Madison to Jefferson, January 22, 1786, in Smith, I, 403.

113 "as distinctly as words can admit . . .": *Detached Memoranda*, in Brenner, 261.

113 "Religion and government . . .": Madison to Edward Livingston, July 10, 1822, in Rakove, 789.

113 "There is not a shadow of right . . .": "General Defense of the Constitution, Virginia Ratification Convention," June 12, 1788, in Brenner, 96.

113 "I am sure that . . .": Madison to Jefferson, October 17, 1788.

114 "Religion. The inefficacy . . .": Madison to Jefferson, October 24, 1787.

114–115 "It was thought not proper . . .": *Detached Memoranda*, in Brenner, 266.

115 "a religious agency . . .": *ibid.*, 265.

115 "seem to imply . . .": *ibid.*

115 "Is not a religious test . . .": Madison to Edmund Pendleton, October 28, 1787, *ibid.*, 91.

116 "Clearly the men . . .": Justice Warren Burger, 1983, *Marsh v. Chambers*.

116 "The establishment of the chaplainship . . .": *Detached Memoranda*, in Brenner, 264.

116 "The Constitution of the U.S. . . .": *ibid.*, 263.

116 "it was not with my approbation . . .": Madison to Edward Livingston, July 10, 1822, in Rakove, 788.

116–117 "If Religion consist . . .": *Detached Memoranda*, in Brenner, 264.

117 "Better also to disarm . . .": *ibid.*, 264.

117 "Could a Catholic . . .": *ibid.*

118 "But besides the danger . . .": *ibid.*, 262–263.

118 "Because the bill in reserving . . .": Madison, "Veto Message to the House of Representatives of the U.S.," February 28, 1811, in Brenner, 199.

119 "Because the bill vests . . .": Madison, "Veto Message to the House of Representatives of the U.S.," February 21, 1811, in Brenner, 198.

119 "A University with sectarian . . .": Madison to Edward Everett, March 19, 1823, in Rakove, 795.

120 "The experience of the United States . . .": Madison to F.L. Schaeffer, December 3, 1821, in Brenner, 357.

120 "Strongly guarded as is the separation . . .": *Detached Memoranda, ibid.*, 262.

120 "old error, that without . . .": Madison to Edward Livingston, July 10, 1822, in Rakove, 788–789.

120 "the people of the United States . . .": the Reverend Jasper Adams, sermon: *The Relation of Christianity to Civil Government in the United States* (Charleston, 1833).

121 "And if we turn . . .": Madison to Jasper Adams, Spring 1833, in Brenner, 395.

CHAPTER SIX: HAMILTON

122 "We look in vain . . .": Henry Cabot Lodge, *Alexander Hamilton* (Boston, 1980), 184.

123 "He had prevailed . . .": Chernow, 481.

124 "Where now, oh! vile worm . . .": cited in Broadus Mitchell, *Alexander Hamilton: Youth to Maturity* (New York, 1957), 665.

125 "Whilst at college . . .": cited in Willard Sterne Randall, *Alexander Hamilton: A Life* (New York, 2003), 73.

126–127 "There is a bigotry . . .": Hamilton, *Second Letter from Phocion* (1784), in Harold C. Syrett, ed., *The Papers of Alexander Hamilton* (New York, 1962), III, 553–554.

127 "There the Jew . . .": Voltaire, *Philosophical Dictionary*, "On the Presbyterians," in *The Portable Enlightenment Reader*, ed. Isaac Kramnick (New York, 1995), 133.

128 "The supposition of universal venality . . .": Hamilton, *Federalist 76*, in Syrett, IV, 637.

128 " . . .The one has no particle . . .": Hamilton, *Federalist 69, ibid.*, 598.

129 "Cherish good faith . . .": Hamilton's draft for Washington's *Farewell Address*, in Syrett, XX, 282–283.

130 "In addition to these . . .": Hamilton to William Loughton Smith, April 10, 1797, *ibid.*, XXI, 41.

131 "[L]et the President recommend . . .": Hamilton to James McHenry, January 27–February 11, 1798, *ibid.*, XXI, 345–346.

131 "In such a crisis . . .": Hamilton to Timothy Pickering, March 22, 1797, *ibid.*, XX, 545.

131–132 "In times like these . . . of the State . . .": *ibid.*, XXIV, 465.

132 "How much, think you . . .": Abraham Bishop, *Connecticut Republicanism: An Oration on the Extent and Power of Political Delusion* (New Haven, 1800), 20.

132–133 "[When] the pretended friends . . .": Bishop, *Oration delivered in Wallingford, Conn.: on the 11th of March 1801, before the Republicans of the State of Connecticut, at their general thanksgiving, for the election of Thomas Jefferson to the presidency, and of Aaron Burr to the vice-presidency, of the United States of America* (Bennington, Vt., 1801), 31.

133 "truly the *Catiline* of America . . .": Hamilton to Oliver Wolcott, December 16, 1800, in Syrett, XXV, 257.

133 "By far not so dangerous . . .": *ibid.*

133–135 "Nothing is more fallacious . . .": Hamilton to James A. Bayard, April 16, 1802, *ibid.*, XXV, 605–610.

135 "The Scruples of a Christian . . .": Hamilton to Elizabeth Hamilton, July 10, 1804, *ibid.*, XXVI, 308.

CHAPTER SEVEN: 1787 AND BEYOND

137 "When the war was over . . .": cited in Boller, 14–15.

139 "liberality . . .": Madison, *Notes on the Debates at the Federal Convention,* ed. Adrienne Koch (Athens, Ohio, 1969), 561.

139 "without much debate . . .": cited in Isaac Kramnick and R. Laurence Moore, *The Godless Constitution: The Case Against Religious Correctness* (New York, 1996), 29.

139 "The door of the Federal Government . . .": *ibid.*, 38.

139 "A Turk, a Jew . . .": cited in Boller, 16.

139 "When I heard . . .": July 30, 1788, *Debates in the Convention of the State of North Carolina on the Adoption of the Federal Constitution*, 198.

140 "Many appear to be much concerned . . .": cited in Jonathan Elliot, ed., *The Debates in the Several State Conventions on the Adoption of the Federal Constitution*, 5 vols. (Philadelphia, 1888), II, 148–149.

140–141 "The civil rights of none . . .": William T. Hutchinson, et al., eds., *The Papers of James Madison* (Chicago, 1962–1969), XII, 201.

141 "No state shall violate . . .": Madison, *ibid.*, 202.

141 "hasten to revise & purify . . .": *Detached Memoranda*, in Brenner, 262.

142 "As the Government . . .": *The Boston Price-Current and Marine Intelligencer*, June 26, 1797.

143 "The nation has offended . . .": cited in Kramnick and Moore, 105–106.

144 "A change has certainly been wrought . . .": John Randolph to Henry Middleton Rutledge, July 24, 1815, in May, 330.

144 "Rousseau, Voltaire . . .": Mrs. Frances Trollope, *Domestic Manners of the Americans* (London, 1832), II, 122.

144 "We, the people . . .": cited in David McAllister, *Christian Civil Government in America* (Pittsburgh, 1927), 21.

145 "The 'establishment of religion' clause . . .": Justice Hugo Black, 1947, *Everson v. Board of Education*.

146 "To declare oneself a nontheist . . .": Kramnick and Moore, 56.

147 "fifth freedom . . .": cited in Naomi Schaefer Riley, *God on the Quad: How Religious Colleges and the Missionary Generation Are Changing America* (New York, 2005), 1.

CHAPTER EIGHT: THE WORLD THAT PRODUCED THE FOUNDERS

149 "the spot of *earth* . . .": Cotton Mather, *Magnalia Christi Americana; or, the Ecclesiastical History of New England*, 2 vols. (1702; reprint, Hartford, 1853), I, 45.

152–153 "The Holy Commonwealth . . .": Lambert, 75.

153–154 "But as the Civill Magistrate . . .": Roger Williams, *The Bloudy Tenet of Persecution* (1644), Chapter 34.

154 "Who hath not found a pallace a prison . . .": cited in Robert S. Alley, *James Madison on Religious Liberty* (Amherst, N.Y., 1985), 133.

156 "Our favorite Doctor Tillotson . . .": Abigail Adams to John Adams, October 20, 1777, in Shuffelton, 317.

156 "Religion and happiness . . .": Lambert, 60.

156 "If an apostle . . .": *ibid.*, 176.

157 "is not a kind of Christianity . . .": Mencken, 95.

157 "The manifest absurdity . . .": Ebenezer Gay, "Natural Religion, as Distinguished from Revealed: A Sermon (Boston, 1759).

158 "a trinity of persons in the godhead . . .": cited in Ann Holt, *A Life of Joseph Priestley* (London, 1931), 140.

158 "the basis of my own faith . . .": Jefferson to Adams, August 22, 1813, in Cappon, 369.

158 "I have even no doubt . . .": Joseph Priestley, *A Letter to the Right Honourable William Pitt*, 2nd ed. (London, 1787), 16–17.

158 "an irreligious and profane man . . .": cited in Richard Brookhiser, *Gentleman Revolutionary: Gouverneur Morris—The Rake Who Wrote the Constitution* (New York, 2003), 128.

158 "The incidents of pleasure and pain . . .": *ibid.*, 184.

159 "denominated a Deist . . .": Ethan Allen, *Reason the Only Oracle of Man, or a Compenduous System of Natural Religion* (Bennington, Vt., 1784), Preface.

159 "The doctrine of the *Incarnation* . . .": Ethan Allen, *Reason the Only Oracle of Man* (New York, 1940), 356.

159 "The doctrine of the Trinity . . .": *ibid.*, 352.

159 "Who in the exercise of reason . . .": *ibid.*, 383.

159 "[T]here could be no justice . . .": *ibid.*, 413.

159 "were previously known . . .": *ibid.*, 192.

160 "Nursery of Bigotry . . .": Milton Klein, ed., *The Independent Reflector or Weekly Essays on Sundry Important Subjects More particularly adapted to the Province of New-York By William Livingston and Others* (Cambridge, Mass., 1963), 204.

160 "Whenever men have suffered . . .": *ibid.*, 316.

160 "'The Old Testament! . . .'": Adams to Benjamin Rush, April 12, 1809, in Schutz and Adair, 157.

161 "Whenever we read . . .": Thomas Paine, *The Age of Reason. Common Sense and Other Writings*, ed. Gordon S. Wood (New York, 2003), 255.

161 "[The New Testament's 'fable'] for absurdity . . .": *ibid.*, 250–252.

161–162 "I believe in one God . . .": *ibid.*, 245.

162 "[H]owever unwilling the partizans . . .": *ibid.*, 275–276.

163 "an incriminating document . . .": Peter Gay, *The Enlightenment: An Interpretation. The Rise of Modern Paganism* (New York, 1995; first published 1966), 87.

164 "In its early history . . .": *ibid.*, 207.

166 "seems to me to be . . .": John Locke, "A Letter Concerning Toleration," in Kramnick, 82.

166 "Now that the whole jurisdiction of the magistrate . . .": *ibid.*, 82–83.

166–167 "If a Roman Catholic believe . . .": *ibid.*, 88.

167 "It does me no injury . . .": Jefferson, *Notes on the State of Virginia*, in Koch and Peden, 254.

167 "[T]he business of laws . . .": Locke, in Kramnick, 88.

167 "Nobody is born . . .": *ibid.*, 85.

167 "why should it not be . . .": *ibid.*

167–168 "[S]eeing one man . . .": *ibid.*, 89.

168 "But if the law . . .": *ibid.*, 90.

168 "mental eruptions . . .": Anthony Ashley Cooper, 3rd Earl of Shaftesbury, in Kramnick, 90.

168 "panic . . .": *ibid.*, 91.

168 "humor . . .": *ibid.*, 93.

168 "of necessity must have vent . . .": *ibid.*

168–169 "It was heretofore the wisdom . . .": *ibid.*

169 "wit . . .": *ibid.*, 95.

169 "raillery . . .": *ibid.*

169 "He who is now an orthodox Christian . . .": Shaftesbury, *Characteristics of Men, Manners, Opinions, Times, etc.*, ed. John Robertson (Gloucester, Mass., 1963), II, 220.

169–170 "'Tis true . . .": Shaftesbury, in Kramnick, 93.

170 "It forms a strong presumption . . .": David Hume, *The Philosophical Works*, eds. Thomas Hill Greene and Thomas Hodge Grose (London, 1882), 96.

170 "[T]he *Christian Religion* . . .": *ibid* ., 108.

170 "If we take in our hand . . .": *ibid.*, 135.

171 "Agitated by hopes and fears . . .": *ibid.*, 316.

171 "The whole is a riddle . . .": *ibid.*, 363.

171 "I see not what bad consequences follow . . .": Hume to James Oswald, in *The Letters of David Hume*, ed. J. Y. T. Greig (Oxford, 1932), I, 106.

172 "Popular superstition and enthusiasm . . .": Adam Smith, *An Inquiry into the Nature and Causes of the Wealth of Nations*, ed. Edwin Cannan (New York, 1994), 852.

172 "[Z]eal must be altogether innocent . . .": *ibid.*, 851–852.

173 "Wholly cast off . . .": Jonathan Edwards, *A History of the Work of Redemption* (Philadelphia, 1773), 281–282.

174 "I conclude all my letters . . .": Voltaire, *Correspondence*, ed. Theodore Bestermann (Geneva, 1953–1965), IL, 138.

174 "Every sensible man . . .": Voltaire, *Oeuvres Competes*, ed. Louis Moland (Paris, 1877–1885), 298.

174 "I believe . . .": cited in Roger Pearson, *Voltaire Almighty: A Life in Pursuit of Freedom* (New York, 2005), 360.

174 "Men are blind . . .": cited in John Bagnall Bury, *A History of Freedom of Thought* (Cambridge, England, 1913), Chapter 6.

175 "What! A ferocious animal . . .": Voltaire, *Oeuvres*, XXVI, 299.

175–177 "Every sect . . .": Voltaire, *Philosophical Dictionary*, "Sect," in Kramnick, 125–127.

177 "contained in four short Words . . .": Adams to Jefferson, December 12, 1816, in Cappon, 499.

177 "The result of our fifty or sixty years . . .": Jefferson to Adams, January 11, 1817, *ibid.*

178 "It has been said before . . .": Voltaire, *Philosophical Dictionary,* "Tolerance," in Kramnick and Moore, 129–130.

178 "Our soul acts internally . . .": Voltaire, *Philosophical Dictionary,* "The Ecclesiastical Ministry," *ibid.*, 116.

178 "The most unlimited liberty . . .": Bury, Chapter 6.

179 "the eternal and immutable truths . . .": Voltaire, *Philosophical Dictionary,* "The Ecclesiastical Ministry," in Kramnick and Moore, 117.

179 "He is virtuous . . .": Claude-Adrien Helvétius, "Treatise on Man," in David George Mullan, ed., *Religious Pluralism in the West: An Anthology* (Oxford and Malden, Mass., 1998), 210.

180 "It is asked . . .": Baron d'Holbach, *Good Sense Without God: Or, Freethinking Opposed to Supernatural Ideas* (Amsterdam, 1772), Article 178.

181 "the most enlightened . . .": Condorcet, *Sketch for a historical picture of the progress of the human mind*, translated by June Barraclough (London, 1955), 174.

181 "offering all the inhabitants . . .": Kramnick, 18.

183 "Science is neither . . .": J. Percy Smith, ed., *Bernard Shaw and H. G. Wells: From the Selected Correspondence of Bernard Shaw* (Toronto, 1995), 10.

A Note on Sources

MY AIM in writing this book was to rely as much as possible on the actual words of the founding fathers themselves. With the exception of Washington, the men treated in this narrative wrote copiously on spiritual and religious subjects, and no original research was called for in communicating their basic attitudes to the reader. Most large libraries contain the writings and papers of these men. For the principal documents of our nation, collected in one volume and chronologically arranged from the seventeenth-century Mayflower Compact and the Virginia Articles, Laws, and Orders to the Lincoln-Douglas debates of 1858, I found *The American Republic: Primary Sources*, edited by Bruce Frohnen (Indianapolis, 2002), to be handy.

A few collections were especially useful to me. First, *The Adams-Jefferson Letters: The Complete Correspondence Between Thomas Jefferson and Abigail and John Adams*, edited by Lester J. Cappon (Chapel Hill, 1959; paperback 1987). The letters exchanged by John Adams and Jefferson, particularly those between 1812 and the death of both men in 1826, are unrivaled windows into the minds of these men and one of the great classics of American literature. Adams also carried on an important correspondence with Benjamin Rush, much of which is excerpted in *The Spur of Fame: Dialogues of John Adams and Benjamin Rush, 1805–1813*, edited by John A. Schutz and Douglass Adair (Indianapolis, 2001). But when writing to Rush, his old crony, Adams often showed his grumpy, partisan side, while in communicating with Jefferson, from whom he had been alienated for years due to their political rivalry, Adams was at his most charming and expansive. Also of interest is Adams's *Journal and Autobiography* (Cambridge, Mass., The Adams Papers, 1962).

Jefferson's papers and letters are filled with thoughts on religion in general and Christianity in particular. The periods of greatest interest here are the 1780s, when he was involved in the battle against religious assessments in Virginia, wrote the Virginia Statute for Religious Freedom, and watched the creation of the Constitution from overseas; and the 1820s, when in old age he finally had the leisure to devote a great deal of thought to the subject of religion. His correspondence with James Madison is especially telling. *Jefferson and Madison on Separation of Church and State: Writings on Religion and Secularism*, edited by Lenni Brenner (Fort Lee, N.J., 2004), is a useful book: Brenner has gathered together in one volume every piece of writing on religion that Jefferson and Madison produced in the course of their lives. It gives a good picture not only of the rather radical religious vision Jefferson and Madison tried to write into law, but of what they were up against: the many conservative Christian statesmen, such as Virginia's Patrick Henry, who were determined to keep Jesus in the government. With his *James Madison on Religious Liberty* (Amherst, N.Y., 1985), Robert S. Alley has brought together pertinent passages from Madison, along with fascinating essays and commentary from various historians and legal scholars.

A quantity of fine books may be found on the general subject of the Founding Fathers and religion. Edwin S. Gaustad, one of the foremost historians of American religion, has edited a two-volume *Documentary History of Religion in America* (Grand Rapids, Mich., 1982). Also of interest are his *Church and State in America* (New York, 1999) and, with Leigh Schmidt, *The Religious History of America: The Heart of the American Story from Colonial Times to Today* (San Francisco, 2004). The Unitarian theologian Forrest Church's *The Separation of Church and State: Writings on a Fundamental Freedom* (Boston, 2002) brings together pertinent texts by many of the founders.

As I have indicated in the text, Isaac Kramnick and R. Laurence Moore's *Our Godless Constitution* (New York, 1996) is an excellent introduction to the subject. Norman Cousins's *In God We Trust: The Religious Beliefs and Ideas of the American Founding Fathers* (New York, 1958) has been an important source for decades, and Gaustad's *Faith of Our Fathers: Religion and the New Nation* (San Francisco, 1987) is very comprehensive. I found Frank Lambert's *The Founding Fathers and the Place of Religion in America* (Princeton, 2003) to be a balanced and informative study. Ronald Hoffman and Peter Albert's *Religion in a Revolutionary Age* (Charlottesville, Va., 1994) is a collection of eleven essays on various aspects of religion in eighteenth-century America. Also of interest are Thomas Curry's *Church and State in America to the Passage of the First Amendment* (New York, 1986), James H. Hutson's *Religion and the Founding of the American Republic* (Washington, D.C., 1998), and Patricia Bonomi's *Under the Cope of Heaven: Religion, Society, and Politics in Colonial America* (New York, 1986). The first two chapters of Susan Jacoby's excellent *Freethinkers: A History of American Secularism* (New York, 2004) deal with colonial and revolutionary America. Franklin Steiner's *The Religious Beliefs of Our Presidents* (Girard, Kans., 1936; reprint 1995) can be read in full on the internet.

There is a great deal of material on the religious beliefs of the six founders treated in this book, with the exception of course of George Washington, who was so very silent on the subject. Paul Boller's *George Washington and Religion* (Dallas, 1963) is a valuable look at the first president. Jefferson's religious ideas are examined in Daniel L. Dreisbach's *Thomas Jefferson and the Wall of Separation Between Church and State* (New York, 2002), and in Edwin S. Gaustad's *Sworn on the Altar of God: A Religious Biography of Thomas Jefferson* (Grand Rapids, Mich., 1996). *The Jefferson Bible: The Life and Morals of Jesus of Nazareth* is available in a pleasing edition (Boston, 1989) with an Introduction by Forrest Church and an Afterword by Jaroslav Pelikan. Alfred O. Aldridge's *Benjamin Franklin and Nature's God* (Durham, N.C., 1967) gives a fair assessment of Franklin's ideas on spirituality and morality. Joseph J. Ellis's *Passionate Sage: The Character and Legacy of John Adams* (New York, 1993) provides as insightful a description of Adams's character as any I have read.

All of Ellis's books, in fact, are of high literary as well as historical quality, and readers of *Moral Minority* will also be interested in his *American Sphinx: The Character of Thomas Jefferson* (New York, 1996) and *His Excellency: George Washington* (New York, 2004). As for general biographies of these six men, there are so many good ones that I have tended to refer most often to the most recent ones, such as Ron Chernow's *Alexander Hamilton* (New York, 2004); David McCullough's *John Adams* (New York, 2001) and John Ferling's *John Adams: A Life* (Knoxville, 1992); Gordon S. Wood's *The Americanization of Benjamin Franklin* (New York, 2004) and Walter Isaacson's *Benjamin Franklin: An American Life* (New York, 2003).

Those who are interested in the long fight for the ratification of the Constitution may look at the sixteen-volume *Documentary History of the Ratification of the Constitution*, ed. Merrill Jensen (Madison, Wisc., 1976), and read about the objections and resistance to it in the six-volume *The Complete Anti-Federalist*, ed. Herbert J. Storing (Chicago, 1981). A valuable one-volume collection of these documents is *The Anti-Federalist Papers and the Constitutional Convention Debates*, ed. Ralph Ketcham (New York, 1986).

For the Enlightenment background and understanding the founders' intellectual formation, I found Henry F. May's *The Enlightenment in America* (New York, 1976) highly useful, also Caroline Robbins's *The Eighteenth Century Commonwealthman* (Cambridge, Mass., 1959) and Trevor Colbourn's *The Lamp of Experience: Whig History and the Intellectual Origins of the American Revolution* (Chapel Hill, 1965). An ideal introduction to the international Enlightenment is Peter Gay's two-volume *The Enlightenment*: vol. 1, *The Rise of Modern Paganism* (London, 1967), and vol. 2, *The Science of Freedom* (London, 1970); a more recent study I found useful is *The Enlightenment and the Intellectual Foundations of Modern Culture* by Louis Dupré (New Haven, 2004). There are countless seventeenth- and eighteenth-century philosophical texts that had a major influence on the founding generation, and it is impossible to go into the subject in much detail here, but readers who are interested should consult, above all, John Locke's *Two Treatises of Government, Letters Concerning Toleration*, and *The Reasonableness of*

Christianity; David Hume's *Enquiry Concerning Human Understanding*, especially the chapter "Of Miracles"; Shaftesbury's *Characteristics of Men, Manners, Opinions, Times, etc.*; a collection of newspaper editorials entitled *Cato's Letters, Or, Essays on Liberty, Civil and Religious, and Other Important Subjects*, by John Trenchard and Thomas Gordon; Henry St. John Bolingbroke's *Dissertation on Parties* and *Letters on the Study of History*; Algernon Sidney's *Discourses Concerning Government*; Samuel Pufendorf's *Of the Nature and Qualification of Religion in Reference to Civil Society*; Voltaire's *Philosophical Dictionary*; and Joseph Priestley's *Letters to a Philosophical Unbeliever* and *History of the Corruptions of Christianity*.

A number of important books bring the concerns of the founders into the present and examine today's religious climate in terms of the past. Notable examples are Noah Feldman's *Divided by God: America's Church-State Problem—and What We Should Do About It* (New York, 2005); Jon Butler, *Awash in a Sea of Faith: Christianizing the American People* (Cambridge, Mass., 1990); and David Cantor's *The Religious Right: The Assault on Tolerance and Pluralism in America* (New York, 1994).

Index

A NOTE ON THE AUTHOR

Brooke Allen grew up in New York City and studied at the University of Virginia and Columbia University, where she received a Ph.D. She then worked in the theater for some years and with wildlife conservation organizations, and as managing editor of *Grand Street* and *Common Knowledge*, both literary quarterlies. Ms. Allen's criticism has appeared frequently in the *New York Times Book Review*, the *Atlantic Monthly*, *The New Criterion*, and the *Hudson Review*, among other publications. Her collections of criticism, *Twentieth-Century Attitudes* and *Artistic License*, were widely praised. She lives in Brooklyn with her husband, the photographer Peter Aaron, and two daughters.